PRAISE FOR STARTUP CE

"A unique perspective distilled from the author's personal journey, both as a former founder CEO himself and from the rich insights he has gained from coaching countless other CEOs in transition.

A must-read for any business leader (and their boards) when navigating the profound shifts of professional transition."

—Leila Rastegar Zegna, General Partner at Kindred Capital

"Imagine someone looking into your soul... This book reveals the innermost secret hopes of founder CEOs and puts them in the context of (tough) reality with kindness and compassion. Much needed, honest, and deeply personal — a must read for every founder CEO."

—Irra Ariella Khi, Founder and CEO of Zamna AI

"Evgeny writes about this subject with intelligence, insight, honesty and sensitivity.

I think it's an outstanding book on an underserved topic and I would strongly recommend it to all leaders whether you're looking to transition, delegate better or simply live a more fulfilled life."

—Simon La Fosse, Executive Chairman
and Founder of La Fosse

"Evgeny's remarkable perspicacity and emotional intelligence sets him apart as a modern business philosopher. This book offers valuable insights and practical advice for founders considering the transition from startup CEO to the next phase of their career."

—Rod Banner, Chair, Investor, and CEO of 3LA.com

"Evgeny has done an amazing job of drawing on his own experience and that of the broader tech ecosystem to examine the complex interaction between founder and CEO roles, how and when to separate them, for your health, well-being and the success of your business. A must-read for founders and investors wanting to better understand founders!"

—Jonathan Lerner, Partner at Smedvig Ventures

"This book was my bible for navigating this major life change. Written by a real expert with great compassion and detail, it's a one-of-a-kind handbook for a niche but totally common reality all CEOs face someday. A must-have."

—Dan Murray-Serter, Co-founder of
Heights and Host at Secret Leaders

"It is not just a straightforward and honest guide to transitioning; it's also an insightful framework for understanding yourself, assessing the reality of where you are as a leader, and making decisions. Having made many successful and very unsuccessful transitions, I wish I'd had this earlier."

—Gi Fernando MBE, Serial Founder and Angel Investor

"An indispensable guide for founders at a crossroads in venture-backed businesses, providing a clear strategy for success."

—Peter Ward, Founder and CEO of Humanity

"It's like a taboo subject that none of us entrepreneurs dare talk about... One day, we might not want to do this anymore, or maybe we want to try something else. Finally, this book shines a light in that dark space and offers a guide on how to navigate it. Most importantly, this book shows us that there is no shame or weakness in wanting to step aside. In fact, we all think about this at some point."

—Alex Depledge, Founder and CEO of Resi

Startup CEO Succession

A Founder's Guide to Leadership Transition

BY EVGENY SHADCHNEV

STARTUP CEO SUCCESSION: A FOUNDER'S GUIDE TO LEADERSHIP TRANSITION

ISBN (hardcover): 978-1-0686430-0-2
ISBN (paperback): 978-1-0686430-1-9
ISBN (eBook): 978-1-0686430-2-6

Published by: Unconditionally Human Ltd
Cover Design by: Lynsey Gray

www.evgeny.coach

To Jerry Colonna,

who showed me the power of radical self-inquiry.

No founder CEO should feel trapped in their job. Much has been written about starting a business, but guidance on stepping away as a CEO of a VC-backed startup is scarce. This is the definitive guide on the emotional and strategic challenges of this transition as a startup leader.

Evgeny Shadchnev draws on firsthand experience of stepping down as founder CEO and as a certified professional coach guiding other CEOs through the same journey. From reflecting on our deepest motivations to choosing the successor and executing a smooth succession plan, Shadchnev helps entrepreneurs and their boards navigate leadership succession when the stakes are highest. It is an essential read for any founder considering this pivotal career transition.

TABLE OF CONTENTS

FOREWORD

The Joy that Dwells Within

For those who've never had the experience, it's terribly hard to understand the emotional challenges of giving up one's seat as a CEO—especially if you're a founder.

I have spent decades counselling, advising, and, even, cajoling CEOs and other leaders—first as an investor and board member and then later as an executive coach. Of all the many, many heart-wrenching and mind-numbing challenges of leadership, nothing compares to the challenge of letting go of the embodiment of your wishes and dreams; a letting go that is so necessary to stepping down from the perch of founding CEO.

And, given his heart, his bravery, as well as his astute observations, it's not surprising that Evgeny Shadchnev has created the best guide to this difficult process I've ever read. For, as he does so often in his work, Evgeny shares from his broken-open warrior heart about his own transition so that he may be of service to those of us going through similar journeys.

Not surprising, I say, and more completely consistent with the man I came to know nearly ten years ago.

I first met Evgeny at one of my coaching company's "boot-camps." For more than a decade, Reboot has hosted dozens of these leadership retreats where struggling entrepreneurs come together to learn new skills, deepen their self-awareness through a process I dubbed "radical self-inquiry," and find kinship and companionship, easing the belief that they alone suffer the crippling self-doubt that so often marks a leaders' journey. I remember two things about our first encounter: his hesitancy around knowing whether he belonged in the room with the other CEOs and his somewhat sad but most-definitely tired eyes.

Later, after knowing him further, I saw his weariness and thought of John O'Donohue's blessing, *For One Who Is Exhausted*:

When the rhythm of the heart becomes hectic,
Time takes on the strain until it breaks;
Then all the unattended stress falls in
On the mind like an endless, increasing weight.

The light in the mind becomes dim.
Things you could take in your stride before
Now become laborsome events of will.

Weariness invades your spirit.
Gravity begins falling inside you,
Dragging down every bone.

The tide you never valued has gone out.
And you are marooned on unsure ground.
Something within you has closed down;
And you cannot push yourself back to life.

You have been forced to enter empty time…

As I read Startup CEO Succession, I thought of our first encounter and the way that poem was received by Evgeny and the other campers. The memory of his tired eyes came back to me as I read of his experience with his crippling, exhausting doubts:

"Why did I want to step down as a CEO myself," he writes. "I had personal and professional reasons. On the personal side, I wasn't looking forward to Monday mornings — or Tuesday mornings, for that matter. Once, my coach asked me to look at my calendar and tell which meetings I dreaded and which I was looking forward to. I opened my calendar and realised I wasn't looking forward to a single meeting that week."

He goes on, "A few years into running the business, I had my first depressive episode that I felt was somehow connected to my work, although I couldn't put my finger on it. I could feel that something was off." Off, and ultimately out of alignment with who he wanted to be.

He then cites several steps he took to fix those feelings. Changing the format of meetings, hiring more experienced managers, meditating, doing yoga—even a trip to a Peruvian jungle for a shaman-led journey with Ayahuasca, were all attempts to get away from the feeling that he was living the wrong life.

"Everything I did helped a bit and gave me a glimmer of hope that one day, I'll fall in love with my job," he writes. But eventually the little bits didn't help; they never added up to the change he desperately needed.

Life, I suspect, became a laborsome event of will.

As Evgeny knew before we even met, I knew such feelings. Indeed, in an effort to help others, I described my own journey through the laborsome events in a recorded talk I delivered in Vienna called *Standing Still While Your Hair Is On Fire*. The dramatic phrase was my attempt to capture the feeling of being seen as successful while living a life that was not yours to live. Evgeny found that recording on YouTube (to this day, I wonder what it was that he was searching for that led him to stumble upon that talk) and decided to come to a bootcamp. I am forever grateful that he did.

I'm grateful for his friendship, of course. But, more, I'm grateful for his book. At our camps, we often speak of "warriors"—brave leaders who have allowed their hearts to be broken open and, in doing so, go first and lead others to be fully present, and thoroughly authentic, with the struggles that are their lives and their jobs. In *Startup CEO Succession*, Evgeny builds on the work that made such a difference in his life in order to give you an understanding that, though scary, such transitions are possible and that the post CEO life can be wonderful.

This is a kind-hearted step-by-step guide to undertaking what is likely to be the most difficult job you'll ever attempt—leaving that which you founded. But by following his example, and bravely leaning into the work, you, too, may emerge not only enlivened once more, but able to help others on a similar journey.

As I think of my friend now I see the ways he is helping others, his eyes, no longer sad but bright, excited, and alive. I see those eyes and am reminded of O'Donohue's assurance that, after learning to rest, the one who is exhausted will gradually return to themselves, "Having learned a new respect for [their] heart and the joy that dwells far within slow time."

May Evgeny's respect for his heart and the joy that dwells within slow time be as helpful to your heart and the easing of your exhaustion as his guide will help you navigate the most important transition of your career.

Jerry Colonna is the founder of Reboot, a leading executive coaching firm. He is also the author of two bestselling books: Reboot: Leadership and the Art of Growing Up *and* Reunion: Leadership and the Longing to Belong.

INTRODUCTION

As a founder CEO of a venture-scale startup, you might feel trapped because you think it's not okay to step down. I'm here to tell you that it's okay. No one is meant to stay in this job forever. In fact, the more successful you are in your job as a founder CEO, the sooner you'll reach a crossroads: either your role will undergo a complete transformation, maintaining the title but overhauling day-to-day responsibilities, or it'll become necessary to bring in a new CEO to elevate the company to greater heights. Both scenarios are marks of success, not failure.

You don't have to feel like a failure if you start thinking about stepping down as a founder CEO. There is a false narrative that people like Jeff Bezos and Mark Zuckerberg are the only role models, going from hiring their first employee and making the first sale all the way to running a global empire. But this is not what happens in the vast majority of companies, and this is not what is suitable for the vast majority of founders.

In fact, stepping down or seriously considering stepping down when your company is either preparing to scale or has scaled to a significant level is perfectly normal. This book will help you decide if you want to step down or stay as a founder CEO, and then get it right the first time if you choose to step down. It will also help you navigate the transition if your board asks you to leave.

In my experience, almost all founder CEOs consider stepping down at some point in their journey. There are various outcomes for startups: some fail, and others are sold, with their founders moving on to different ventures. However, many startups exist in a middle ground: valuable and growing, yet not ready for immediate sale or an IPO. In many companies, founders often reassess their priorities after years of hard work, especially as their personal life changes, such as starting a family or when it becomes clear that the business would benefit from a different leader.

This book is a guide on the succession of startup founders. Drawing from my own experiences as a founder CEO and then as a coach to other founders, I offer a unique framework for navigating this transition. A lot has been written about starting a company, but guidance on how to step down as a founder CEO is scarce. Yet, how you and your board approach this process can create or destroy millions of pounds of value. Whether and how you step down are among the most consequential decisions you'll make as the CEO of your startup.

WHO THIS IS FOR

You may be a founder of a venture-scale company, navigating the challenges and complexities of running a startup. Or maybe you're a venture capitalist, a board member, or an incoming CEO looking to understand the process from the founder's perspective.

This book is particularly relevant for founder CEOs who are contemplating stepping down or who have been advised to do so by their board, and board members. It offers insights and guidance from the unique perspective of a founder CEO, which is valuable for anyone involved or interested in this transition.

WHY I WROTE THIS BOOK

As a founder of Makers, a London-based VC-backed startup, this is the book I needed when I was considering stepping down as a CEO. For too long, I felt trapped in my role, feeling unable to leave but not enjoying running the business. Even admitting my doubts felt like a failure. Doesn't every founder want to stay at the helm forever?

I didn't plan to become a CEO. I remember my co-founder Rob calling me and saying he was struggling with a long-distance relationship with his wife, who had recently moved to Germany. That wasn't news to me, but at that moment, I could feel that Rob wasn't just struggling. Having a choice between a startup in London and family in Germany, Rob had to focus on the family, even though he probably hadn't admitted it to himself yet.

In the following weeks, Rob decided to step down as CEO, and we agreed that I'd take over from him. I didn't plan to become a CEO, but the company needed a leader, and I was the only remaining co-founder.

We formalised it at the next board meeting and told the team. Our startup was just over one year old, and the team was under ten people. As far as CEO transitions go, that one was simple.

Not all CEO transitions are straightforward. Many years later, when Makers was a more established business, I stepped down as a CEO myself. When I committed to the transition, the company was seven years old, with a team of over 60 full-time employees.

By then, we had trained thousands of software engineers, raised a few million of venture capital and venture debt to finance our growth and established Makers as a well-respected tech training provider in the UK, helping some of the country's leading companies hire diverse and capable tech professionals.

This time, the CEO transition was more complex. First, it took me a long time to decide to replace myself as a CEO. Second, there were more moving parts and only one shot at getting it right.

As a CEO, I made plenty of mistakes, but I am proud of how we, as the board, handled the transition from me to the new leader. The company is in a better place under the leadership of Claudia Harris OBE, who took over from me as the CEO of Makers, and I am much happier with the next stage of my career as a founder coach.

Working with dozens of founder CEOs in transition as their coach, I learned I was far from the only person facing two questions. First, how do you decide to step down as a founder CEO? Second, how do you get it right the first time?

WHAT'S AT STAKE?

Do you really need to read yet another book on startups? Isn't your bookshelf already bursting with books you intended to read and maybe even started but never finished? Which founder has time to read all of them anyway?

The reason for reading this particular book is what's at stake. A CEO transition in a startup can create or ruin millions and millions of pounds of value and lead to sleepless (or restful!) nights years down the line. Your decisions during the transition will influence how and where you retire, even if this moment is decades away. What you decide now will also impact your future career opportunities.

During the founder CEO succession, what's at stake is a material amount of value for all shareholders and, more importantly, the founder's peace of mind.

You'll face choices with non-obvious consequences at every stage of this transition. To step down or to stay? Is your desire to leave a moment of weakness, or is stepping down precisely what needs to happen for you and your business to thrive? Who will be your successor? Will that person lead the business to success or failure? What's next for you? Will you repeat the same unconscious patterns from the past or see through them and take a bold step into the unknown future?

As a founder CEO, you make countless decisions as part of your job. You forget most of them the following day. However, the decision of whether, how and when to step down is one of those that you'll remember long after you leave.

WHAT WE SHALL COVER

We will explore the intricate and often challenging process of transitioning from a founder CEO to a new leader. Drawing upon my extensive experience coaching numerous founder CEOs, I've realised that the questions surrounding the decision to step down and the subsequent transition are not unique. Each journey, while distinct, shares common threads and invaluable lessons.

The book is divided into nine chapters, corresponding to nine steps of this journey, from understanding why you want to leave all the way to deciding what to focus on next in your career.

No doubt, you will find some steps easier than others. For some founders, making the decision is the most challenging step, but executing it is easy. Other founders clearly want to step down and know why but struggle for years to find a successor they have confidence in. Yet others may hesitate to commit to the transition because they don't know how to overcome their fears.

Still, everyone will have to go through all nine steps on their journey, from first considering stepping down to entering the next stage of their professional life.

UNDERSTAND YOUR REASONS FOR STEPPING DOWN

The first chapter looks at the hidden drivers behind your desire to leave. You need clarity on some big, personal questions to know how to approach the rest of the CEO transition. Why did you start your business? What are you really meant to be doing? Who are you, deep inside? And, what might you be running away from?

WORK THROUGH YOUR FEARS

Next, we look at the emotional aspects of leaving the company you founded. This chapter outlines common fears and anxieties that founder CEOs face, such as fear of losing identity, concerns about the company's future, and the uncertainty of what lies ahead. We will discuss strategies to accept and manage these fears, which are a natural part of the process.

ASSESS YOUR SITUATION

Once you have found clarity on what prompted you to consider stepping down and looked at the fears that might be holding you back, you'll need to look at the practical circumstances of your life. How strong is your skillset, and what does the business need? How sound are your personal finances? How will stepping down (or staying in your job) affect your family?

MAKE THE DECISION

Then, we talk about the importance of being decisive before discussing different options available to you, such as returning money to investors or selling the business. Our aim is to make a decision you are confident in, regardless of what you decide to do.

KICK OFF THE PROCESS

Once you make the decision to step down, you'll need to choose how to share it with other people, starting with the board, in a way that maintains trust and optimises the timing of the transition. Trust at the board level is one of the key drivers of the success of any CEO succession, so the conversation with the board should be approached carefully.

CHOOSE YOUR SUCCESSOR

This chapter discusses the importance of choosing a successor who aligns with the company's vision and culture. We will cover identifying potential candidates, evaluating their skills and leadership styles, and the considerations for an internal versus external appointment.

PREPARE A SMOOTH TRANSITION

Here, we cover practical aspects that can ensure a smooth transition of leadership. This includes clarifying your responsibilities and getting out of the way of the new CEO to avoid undermining them. At the same time, it's important to think through legal and financial considerations of the transition, such as rebalancing the cap table and negotiating the exit package for the outgoing CEO. We'll also discuss how to break the news to the world and say goodbye to the team you led for years.

REST AND REFLECT ON YOUR CAREER OPTIONS

In this section, we explore the opportunities and challenges that lie ahead for you after stepping down. However tempting it may be to rush into the next stage of your professional life, this transition will benefit from slowing down and reflecting on what matters to you in life and where you want to take your career next.

CHOOSE YOUR NEXT PROFESSIONAL STEP

Lastly, we examine the stories of other founder CEOs who have successfully navigated this journey. By sharing their experiences, challenges, and outcomes, their real-life insights and lessons will help you through your own transition. Whether you start another business, get a corporate job or become an investor, the stories of others who walked this path will help you choose the right next step for you.

WHAT YOU CAN EXPECT

This book will help you confidently decide if you should step down, and if so, execute it with grace and poise, putting a great new leader in charge of the business you started before moving on to the next stage of your career.

It is often said that being a CEO is a lonely job. I know this is true from personal experience and working with many other founders as their coach. The process of leaving your CEO job feels particularly lonely. Yet, it doesn't have to be this way. Countless founders faced the same questions and fears you are facing and have found a way forward.

This book is a guide to accompany you on every stage of this journey.

CHAPTER 1

UNDERSTAND YOUR REASONS FOR STEPPING DOWN

Most founder CEOs consider stepping down at some point, often more than once. It is essential to start our exploration focused on your inner world, looking for clarity around why you want to step down. This is, perhaps, the most crucial step because it will influence how you approach the conversation with the board, the choice of successor, and your next professional endeavour.

If you're like most founders considering stepping down, you have many questions in your mind and some complex emotions, too. This is normal. We're looking for clarity on what you really want, what you're meant to be doing and what psychological pain you might be trying to avoid by building a startup. The best way to do this is by examining a series of questions that bring you more clarity — which I have outlined in this chapter.

After all, there's no algorithm to get the answers you need by following a set of instructions. I know because I have struggled with these questions myself. I hope my journey, shared in this chapter, will help you find the clarity you need. In the following chapter, we will explore common fears experienced by founders in transition.

WHAT INSPIRED YOU TO BUILD A STARTUP?

"Why did you start your business?" I asked my super-successful boss as we were riding in a taxi, returning from a late-night business function. I was a junior software developer with zero business experience. Still, I was curious about what inspired him to build an innovative, incredibly profitable company that was a fun place to work. Surely, there was some grand dream behind it?

"I wanted to make money," he said. "I got my first job after uni, making twenty-something grand a year, and I couldn't afford to go out. That's all."

In the couple of decades since, I have asked this question to countless founders, friends and coaching clients. Everyone has a different story. Some wanted to get rich. Some wanted to make a dent in the universe. Some wanted to get famous. Some wanted to get powerful. And some just wanted their Dad to praise them, finally, instead of telling them to try harder. They wanted to feel loved.

There is no right or wrong answer to this question, but each answer matters greatly. We can't jump straight to understanding the reasons for leaving without understanding where it all started, often going back to our early career and the story of our family.

In my twenties, I thought I wouldn't amount to anything unless I started a successful business. I wasn't sure what success meant to me or what exactly I was trying to amount to, but like many people at the early stages of their careers, I was eager to prove myself, and I thought that building a business would be "it".

Naively, my co-founder and I thought that we'd build something to sell in 2-3 years – our initial idea was to "get an exit" rather than to build a successful business – but one year in, we realised it would be a much longer journey. Building an unsuccessful startup often takes years before the founders run out of money and ideas. A successful one can easily take a decade or more before there's an exit.

However, once we started placing the developers we trained into their first jobs in technology, I realised that helping people change their careers and lives was much more meaningful than our original plan to flip the business quickly.

I remember talking to one developer we trained who shared, tearfully, how much she loved working as a software developer for a leading financial publication in the UK. Her entire life, she explained, she believed that 'work has to suck but must be done to pay the bills'.

Seeing her tears of joy helped me realise what we were building was far more meaningful than a quick exit. Creating a commercially viable business is a success, but building one where your customers regularly describe their experience as "life-changing" is a privilege.

I'm proud to have founded a business that counts Apple, Google, Deloitte, Microsoft, several branches of the UK government, The Financial Times and hundreds of other outstanding companies as its clients. I love seeing how our students go from writing their first line of code to getting their first job, getting their first promotion, running their first team, getting their first CTO job, or starting their own tech startup, as many have done.

This impact on the lives of our customers and the UK tech ecosystem as a whole often made me doubt if I should step down. Was I not running a great business making a meaningful difference in the world?

This is the predicament many founders find themselves in. On the one hand, the business we built is doing great, and we can list plenty of reasons we should be happy running it. On the other hand, we aren't happy running it, regardless of what we think we should feel. Or maybe we feel we can't step down, even if we know we can. Clearing up this confusion has to be the start of our journey.

HOW ALIGNED DO YOU FEEL DEEP INSIDE?

Why did I step down as a CEO myself? I had personal and professional reasons. On the personal side, I wasn't looking forward to Monday mornings – or Tuesday mornings, for that matter. Once, my coach asked me to look at my calendar and tell which meetings I dreaded and which I was looking forward to. I opened my calendar and realised I wasn't looking forward to a single meeting that week.

That was clear, but understanding why took some time. A few years into running the business, I had my first depressive episode that I felt was somehow connected to my work, although I couldn't put my finger on it. I could feel that something was off, and it was incredibly tempting to fix that.

So, I started looking for things to fix. If I hated running the senior team meetings, I tried to change the format. I hired more experienced executives. I took holidays and exercised. I read management books. I meditated and practised yoga. I delegated aggressively to focus on what only I could do. Over the years, I have worked with several different founder coaches.

I went to the Peruvian jungle to see if Ayahuasca — a powerful plant medicine with psychedelic effects used in shamanic ceremonies by indigenous people— would make it easier to understand what was going on and why I really didn't like leading a successful, mission-driven business that was changing customer lives. (Mother Ayahuasca told me I should stay as a CEO, but two months later, I already doubted her opinion. After all, she never ran a startup.)

Everything I did helped a bit and gave me a glimmer of hope that one day, I'd fall in love with my job. Yet, that day always felt a few months away. Given that our mission at Makers is to help people transition into a career they love, not being in love with my job felt hypocritical.

Understanding the reasons behind how I felt was important because, if I didn't uncover them, I would end up in another job I didn't like. We are condemned to repeat the patterns we are not aware of. To change them, we need to bring them to light.

James Routledge, founder of Sanctus, reflects on his experience of stepping down as a CEO:

> "The hardest thing to do is just be really, really honest with yourself. Brutally honest about what you want. And really notice where you might be censoring yourself. Whatever practices you can do to be really honest with yourself, whether that's coaching, therapy, journaling, spending time alone in nature — whatever it is, it is critical to be really honest with yourself."

One of my most memorable holidays when I was a CEO was a solo motorbike trip along the coast of Scotland, followed by a meditation retreat. One day, somewhere deep in the beautiful Scottish countryside, I was sitting by a loch watching ducks play in the water when a simple realisation struck me: I don't have to fight, strive, or achieve to be happy.

That moment was perfect as it was. I watched the clouds and birds. I noticed a slight feeling of hunger and was perfectly okay with it all. I was complete.

A couple of weeks later, I was sitting opposite my coach in London, trying and failing to explain how right that moment felt and how wrong it felt to be back to my job. It wasn't simply about being idle or resting; it was more profound than that. In that moment, deep down, I was much more aligned with who I am than when I had ever been as a CEO.

What was the message there? What was the lesson I needed to learn from that experience? I could feel that it was essential that my inner being was aligned with what I did. Also, I felt my work must be an expression of who I am as a person in order to be good.

I really wanted to feel alignment inside, but my work didn't give me that feeling. To confuse things, the feedback from my chair and the board was generally positive. I was not a perfect CEO, but I wasn't failing at my job. On the inside, however, I rarely felt like I was succeeding.

In the early years of running Makers, I felt aligned with what I did and how I did it. I might have been deluded in thinking I needed to build a successful business to feel validated or loved, but that's what I thought then, so I worked hard to build the business. I might have been utterly exhausted, but I also felt unstoppable in my delusion.

As founders, we have big dreams. We want to make life-changing inventions, make lots of money, achieve fame or recognition, and impact the world, but there's also a much deeper psychological dimension at play. As human beings, we want to be safe, loved, and feel like we belong.

Often, and that was my case, we develop elaborate and usually subconscious strategies to feel the way we want. Maybe deep inside, we don't feel accepted, but we hope that being successful will make us feel this way. Maybe deep inside, we feel we aren't worthy, but we hope that making a significant, positive impact on the world will make this feeling disappear.

This psychological drive often pushes us to build world-changing businesses and also helps us recognise that external achievements don't lead to lasting happiness. Still, external accomplishments and impact on the world matter. Hopefully, along the way, we realise that we are enough as we are. This realisation can completely change our motivation for doing our work and take it in a different direction.

A few years after founding the business, I couldn't avoid the conclusion that I had changed. More precisely, I became more aware of how I was deluding myself, trying to plug a hole inside by building a business. There's more to life than building a successful business. What I do must be aligned with who I am. I don't have to strive and fight to feel okay. I am enough as I am. But who am I?

Living this question gradually started taking more and more of my attention. Something in my being — call it soul, call it spirit — was striving to be itself and express itself. More and more of my experience was shifting from doing to being.

I became increasingly aware that whatever was trying to express itself through me didn't look like running a venture-backed startup transforming the tech industry's future. The more I forced myself to be someone I was not and do things that weren't unfolding naturally, the more I suffered.

And, of course, there was fear. It's one thing to feel like one way of life is not serving you when you know what's coming next. It's quite another when you know you're in the wrong place and must let go of one trapeze before catching the other. Being a founder isn't just a job but part of your identity. What if I don't catch the other trapeze? Where is it anyway?

Yet, before there was clarity on what was next for me, I was sure there was a significant and growing disconnect between what was trying to express through me and what I did for a living. Something inside me was shouting louder and louder, trying to be heard. Starting to listen to that part of me was finally the first step towards healing.

There were also professional reasons why stepping down was right for me. As the CEO, my primary responsibility was to steward the company towards success. As we were growing and signing up more impressive enterprise clients, I needed to keep evolving my skill set to meet large clients' needs, delivering an increasingly complex set of products as a regulated business. The company needed a CEO who deeply understood the needs of B2B clients and wanted to make this job their primary focus for the next few years. And that differed from the direction in which I felt I was being taken.

I'm deliberately using a passive voice here ("being taken") rather than an active voice ("I chose to take") because of a growing sense that before telling my life what I wanted it to be, I needed to listen and hear what plans it had for me.

Parker Palmer reflects beautifully on this in his book *Let Your Life Speak,* in which he describes his own journey of trying to be this and that, bouncing from one vocation to the next, until he started to listen to what his life was telling him about who he is and what he's meant to be doing.

This is a delicate balance between listening and taking action. We need both. If we act without listening to our lives, we'll try to build a life that doesn't serve us. It might look beautiful on the outside, but we'll feel dead inside. If we listen without acting, we might not get much done.

There's a place here for both intelligence and wisdom. Intelligence is the ability to achieve your goals. Wisdom is knowing which goals are worth achieving. We need both equally, as if they were two wings supporting a bird in the sky.

Staying in my role as a CEO, knowing that my soul was not aligned with the work I needed to do, would have been a disservice to the company and a violation of integrity. The company deserved a different CEO. And I needed to let go of the trapeze I was holding for the other trapeze to appear.

Describing my choosing to step down as some sophisticated spiritual choice that I reflected on while watching ducks in Scotland doesn't do justice to what it felt like at the moment. The day-to-day reality of running a startup can feel like, to use the words of executive coach Jerry Colonna, "standing still while your hair is on fire."

Sometimes, I was able to stand still and feel my hair burning. Other times, I felt like I was breaking down — like the day I woke up crying at 5 am after a tough senior management team meeting.

Yet, the fact that it felt hard wasn't the problem per se. Lots of things in life are hard. Life is full of pain, big and small. We don't have some God-given right to be free from pain. On the contrary, everyone is guaranteed some, starting the second we're born.

However, there's a difference between demanding challenges we want to rise to and those that are demanding but not ours to meet. Leading Makers for the next decade was not the right challenge for me.

An exploration of why we may feel like it's time to step down as a founder CEO cannot stop only at the question of what's not working. To find clarity in such a situation, we must also enquire about what we're meant to be doing right now.

WHAT ARE YOU MEANT TO BE DOING?

When working with founders as a coach, I am curious about their circumstances: financial goals, family commitments or stress levels, which we will discuss later in the book. However, I'm especially curious about what they feel they are meant to be doing right now.

I'm unashamedly spiritual about it. We habitually feel as if we are masters of our destiny, and to an extent, it's true. Choices that we make lead to consequences that we experience. This entire book is about making one big choice.

And yet, it's not the whole story. We're also unique individuals with our own distinct conditioning, skills, hopes, dreams and desires. Like waves in the ocean, we're simultaneously unique and alike. Our distinctiveness meets our life circumstances, resulting in an unrepeatable expression we experience as a self and call "I".

Whatever we feel we choose to do, there's also a vital force of life working to express itself, whether we want it or not. We are not nearly as separate from the rest of life as we usually feel.

In the stillness of meditation, we notice that even when we resolve to do nothing for the duration of the session, thoughts, moods, impulses, desires, and experiences are still present. We're unfolding in every moment, just like a flower grows and changes every second.

What is trying to be expressed through you? Allow yourself to forget what you think you want or need for a second. What work are you meant to do in this world? What is trying to be born through you?

There's little point in trying to answer these questions intellectually as if we were deciding whether to have scrambled eggs or granola for breakfast. Instead, we need to listen to the answer by staying present to our feelings, allowing complex emotions to rise to the surface and seeing through our mind's attempts to "save" us from unpleasant feelings by coming up with a clever but misguided strategy.

Only then, when we learn to accept and feel our feelings and understand which behaviours stem not from our authentic selves but from our attempts to avoid pain, will we be ready to see what emerges when we ask, "What am I meant to be doing in this world?"

It's a scary question because there's a chance that the answer won't look like "the CEO of my startup". And yet, it's an indispensable question because to live a good and fulfilled life, you must be aligned with what's trying to express itself through you. To be a great CEO, you need to feel, deep down, that that's what you're meant to be doing right now.

Not only is the question scary, but the answer is never final. We need to give up the fantasy of finding our most profound and authentic purpose once and for all. Instead, we must learn to live with uncertainty, asking this question occasionally to see if the answer changes, as it surely will.

One of the reasons the answer changes is that we ourselves change dramatically throughout our lives. How the world looks to us when we're teenagers or young adults will undoubtedly evolve once we start a family and accept responsibility for others. It may change once again once we start transitioning into the second half of life when we begin reevaluating what ultimately matters to us and what really drives us.

It may still feel unbearably difficult at times, even if you're confident that being the CEO of your business is what you're meant to be doing right now. I think of one of my clients, a bootstrapped founder, who's well familiar with the difficulty of getting a SaaS company off the ground without investment. When we meet when it's especially tough for him, I notice that he'd rather be anywhere else in the world but in his CEO chair, and yet he wouldn't trade his role for anything.

Like an athlete exerting themselves past the point of exhaustion and yet choosing to compete in the Olympics, he feels the pain and decides to face it anyway. Just because you think you're meant to do this work doesn't mean it will be an easy ride.

Every CEO trying to understand what they are meant to be doing knows the answer deep down. Instead of being found, it needs to be heard. That answer will be whispered in quietness when the voices of pain and ambition quieten down, as it happened to me as I was sitting by the side of a loch in Scotland.

Over the years, I learned this voice has a quiet and calm demeanour. It's not tainted by the drive of adrenaline, which tells me that I am strong enough to go through the pain of building a startup. It's not distorted by the voice of fear, which tells me it's too difficult, unpredictable, and nauseating.

That voice is calm and grounded. It says, matter-of-factly, without trying to persuade or cause drama: you are meant to be doing this right now. Or maybe it says that you aren't.

Either answer is okay. It's great news, regardless of the answer, because having access to this quiet, grounded feeling gives us the clarity we need to move forward.

This feeling of clarity is what you are looking for if you're starting to contemplate the big question. It is different from adrenaline-fuelled excitement or fear-driven anxiety. It's an inner calm where you can weigh up different options and feel at peace with whatever conclusion you come to.

Inner calm and conviction can help us see through our ego telling us that we shouldn't be doing something because it's scary. Sometimes, the ego can feel deficient if it doesn't get whatever it wants. However, the ego doesn't last long in silence. In stillness, it fades, and its desires disappear like dreams upon waking up.

The feeling familiar to many is that we're an impostor in our jobs, waiting to be found out by others who, we assume, actually know what they're doing. This feeling can't survive in the inner calm when we slow down. Inevitably, slowing down either helps us connect with our inner strength or realise, without unnecessary drama, what we should be doing instead.

Slowing down helps us feel the difference between wanting and longing. They have different energies. Wanting is a feeling that arises from a place of lack when we think that we aren't complete or enough unless we get something. Wanting is personal: we strongly feel like separate individuals who want to get something. Wanting comes from the mind that says, "I want that".

Our wants and desires are fleeting. Our desires can feel irresistible until we get distracted by something. To want something is human, but noticing how it's different from longing is essential.

Longing comes from a place of wholeness and completeness. Its energy is more grounded and calm, without a craving feeling that comes with wanting something badly. Longing comes from a place of hope and optimism, rooted in a vision of a better world.

Longing is born in the heart, not the mind. It comes from something more profound than our rational thoughts and persists in time, calling, but not driving, us towards a higher ground. Longing feels less personal than wanting. My ego wants many things, but it doesn't long for anything. That's the heart's job.

Whatever you're meant to do, part of you longs for it. You may or may not want it. What you long for may be downright scary for the ego, but that's the ego's job: to be a bit scared and greedy. The answer to what you're meant to be doing will be found in the place of longing and surrender deep in your heart.

WHAT ARE YOU RUNNING AWAY FROM?

We sometimes do what we aren't meant to because we are running away from something we are unwilling to acknowledge. We may believe we are deficient in some way, which evokes some uncomfortable feelings. Then, our minds, usually unconsciously, devise a strategy to ensure we don't ever feel these feelings, which may well include building a startup.

In such situations, a founder may feel permanently stuck, like they aren't in the right place but can't quit for reasons they can't easily explain.

One of my earliest memories from when I must have been around three years old is going out to play in my grandparents' courtyard. They lived in a large block of flats, and local kids had a playground they could enjoy while being watched from dozens of balconies and windows over them. I saw some kids I didn't know and tried to approach them, but they started teasing me instead.

As small children, we don't yet have the emotional maturity to experience intense feelings without being overwhelmed. When we experience pain interacting with others as children, we tend to conclude that there's something wrong with us. If these kids didn't want to play with me, I thought, there must have been something wrong with me, and if they ran away from me, there must have been something repulsive about me.

In hindsight, I realise that social rejection was one of my formative experiences, later reinforced at school, where I constantly felt like I wasn't fitting in, but desperately wanted to be accepted by my classmates. At the same time, I knew that I was different from them in some important ways, and they were not my tribe.

After many hours of therapy and self-reflection, I connected the dots as an adult, seeing clearly to what extent my desire to be accepted, respected and loved by others has been driving my life choices.

That subconscious desire to find my tribe, people I like and respect, and to be liked and accepted by them eventually led me to the startup community. As a computer science student and a geek at heart, I felt for the first time in my life that the founder community was where I belong, or at least should belong.

Feeling, but not acknowledging, that sense of deficiency I first felt as a three-year-old, I decided I needed to build a startup.

What I didn't know was that I was running away from feeling rejected and deficient as a small child, quietly hoping, in my unconscious mind, that if I built a successful business, I wouldn't ever have to feel that way again. I would be able to relax and finally feel okay. I would feel loved, accepted, and respected for who I am.

Not being aware of this dynamic created the double bind I found myself in. Being a founder was the mechanism I relied on to feel that I belonged to a tribe of people I respect while not feeling rejected and teased. At the same time, a part of me knew that being a CEO was not what I was meant to do. That's why it was a double bind: whatever I did, I felt I would either sacrifice my integrity or face the feelings I wasn't yet ready to feel.

Yet that understanding of what I was running away from eventually helped me to start asking different questions. What if I can be respected and accepted just as I am without a business card saying "Founder and CEO"? What if I can face those scary feelings from childhood and discover they are not dangerous? What if I can feel okay without compromising my integrity?

The curious thing about feelings is that they don't harm us when we feel them. They only harm us (and others) when we aren't willing to feel them and enact neurotic strategies to avoid them.

Understanding what we are running away from and facing it can help us determine whether we need to be running away in the first place. If our startup is an elaborate running away strategy, we might do ourselves a favour by asking if all of that is necessary to feel fundamentally okay.

Being aware of how you're feeling in the moment and being able to stay with it without any attempt to change how you feel is a skill. Like any other skill, it can be learned. Without it, we are at the mercy of our automatic reactions and habits that run our lives when we are not paying attention.

It is challenging but indispensable to do this work while still under the pressure of running a startup. We need to slow down and look at the pattern of our activity and feelings, connecting the dots between how we might have felt in childhood and what we're doing today as adults. Childhood is often the right starting place because that's where our life strategies are first conceived, surviving into adulthood, and often well past the time when they are helpful.

There are countless ways to get started on this journey. Talking or somatic therapy, yoga, coaching, journalling, circling, meditation, bodywork, and numerous other modalities can all help us get to know ourselves better in the safety of a trusted relationship. However, what's important is that we start exploring what we're afraid of and then keep moving forward without any rush when we inevitably encounter things inside that we don't want to be there.

WHAT'S KEEPING YOU FROM HAPPINESS?

Running away from our feelings isn't the only way to make life choices that aren't aligned with who we are deep inside. Elaborate fantasies of future life when we finally arrive and become happy also play a big part.

For founders, as undoubtedly was the case for me, it usually takes the form of dreaming about a massive exit, followed by lots of free time to finally do all the things that founders are too busy to do, including maybe buying some fancy properties or expensive toys.

Or, perhaps the dream is to become an angel investor or an LP in a venture fund, to spend the days looking for the most promising ideas and founding teams (being secretly grateful it's not you who's going to be working very hard for years to make the vision a reality).

In my case, I was entertaining a fantasy of selling the business and moving from London to Chamonix in the French Alps to hike and paraglide during the summer and sit by a warm fireplace with a book and a glass of hot wine during dark winter evenings.

This dream was helping me escape the reality of the moment and ignore the growing feeling that I should be doing something else. It's almost as if the dream was saying, "Don't worry, you can forget how you feel right now because once you sell the business, you'll finally become happy."

This was a blatant lie, of course. The truth is that we can never become happy; we can only be happy. And while there's nothing wrong with running a business, selling a business, staying where you are or moving elsewhere, entertaining dreams of future happiness could be precisely what keeps us stuck in the present misery.

I see this with the stories my clients are telling me. One dreams of buying a mansion in southern Europe while wondering how many more years he can endure doing a job he doesn't like on a below-market salary. Another client dreams about a new startup he'll start once he's done with his current one – a bootstrapped, profitable, growing business building innovative products that customers want.

I'm also thinking about several clients who made life-changing money when they sold their businesses, only to find themselves lost. Without the financial need to work for someone else or build another company, they faced the task of discovering who they were and what they wanted to do with their life. This is important and necessary work, but it is not what they expected to do after the exit.

We need goals and dreams, of course. But we should be careful not to use them as an excuse to live someone else's life for the time being. A successful startup can easily take a decade or more to build. An unsuccessful one might take less time but even more stress.

As founders trying to decide whether to quit, we might ask ourselves whether we would be happy to keep running this business indefinitely. Of course, we won't — no job lasts forever — but asking this question can prompt us to change our circumstances, reflect on our attitude or get out of the way.

It's important not to hide behind the "I'll be happy when..." story because it undermines our well-being, prevents us from being happy and fulfilled right now and doesn't allow us to be the best CEOs we can be.

To do a great job, the job itself must be the reward, not the means to an end. And your startup will only be very successful if the CEO does a great job.

At the heart of it all, a founder CEO wants to be satisfied with their life and do an excellent job. These two things are closely related. To be a great CEO, we need to know that this is what we are meant to do with our life right now, not be running away from something or entertaining tantalising fantasies of future happiness.

Reflecting on all these big questions isn't meant to be easy or fun. Moreover, doing it in one afternoon or one weekend is impossible. It's equally impossible to cover all possible questions that must be explored in a single chapter.

Yet, this work is indispensable if we are to understand deeply why we're considering stepping down. This work must be done over many conversations with trusted friends and confidants and hours of solitude and reflection. The more clarity we have at this stage, the easier it will be to orchestrate a good transition.

The outcome you seek is a sense of clarity on who you are, what matters deeply to you, why you started the business, and what has changed in the years since. This work is needed to understand why you may feel like stepping down as the CEO of the company you started.

This is less about making an intellectual argument and more about a sense of clarity that arises when we slow down to reflect deeply on who we are and what we really want.

Questions to reflect on:

- What drives me to wake up every morning and work on my business?
- Which aspects of my past am I attempting to rewrite or improve through my entrepreneurial journey?
- What vision am I working towards that feels out of reach as long as I'm a CEO?
- In what ways does my business serve as a distraction from confronting personal truths?
- What unexplored passion keeps resurfacing in my thoughts, suggesting a different direction?

CHAPTER 2

WORK THROUGH YOUR FEARS

I've yet to meet a founder who doesn't have some fears related to stepping down as CEO. When you started the process of self-inquiry outlined in the previous chapter, looking into your dreams, hopes, and fantasies, you undoubtedly came across things that might have frightened you. This chapter explores some of the most common fears founders face.

What you are looking for is not to remove the fears but to get to know them. Looking closely at our fears and learning to stay with them, we inevitably realise that they are not as scary as they seem. The goal is to get to know our fears so well that we become comfortable in their presence.

By looking at a few common fears, we'll see that none of them are as scary as they initially seem. Then, we'll be ready to embark on the rest of our journey, not without fears but with a sense of trust in our abilities to handle what life has to offer.

Getting to know our fears will make all the difference when we start looking at the practical circumstances of your situation in the following chapter. What may look like a threat when a fear is denied might appear as an opportunity when the same fear is acknowledged and welcomed.

WHAT IF I'M MAKING A MISTAKE?

My own biggest fear was that I was trying to solve the wrong problem. As much as I felt that I wasn't aligned with what I was doing in some essential ways, the subversive voice in my head sarcastically asked me, "Are you sure whatever you choose to do next will be more aligned with your true self? How do you know that it's the right step to take? Wouldn't it make more sense to find an opportunity to exit the business instead of stepping down?"

After all, my life as the CEO of Makers was so comfortable in many ways. I loved the company, the team, and the mission. I'm genuinely proud of the Makers' positive impact on the UK tech industry and the lives of thousands of people we trained, one of whom even tattooed our logo on his wrist when he got a job as a software developer.

As CEO, I was supported by the board, which didn't try to tell me how to run the business. I wasn't too worried about money, had all the flexibility I needed to work in a way that suited me and grew professionally with every new challenge we navigated as a team. Autonomy, mastery, purpose—couldn't I put a tick to each of those?

I asked myself whether I was solving the real problem or barking up the wrong tree. Since the decision to step down as the CEO of the company you founded is generally irreversible, it's worth acknowledging this fear and articulating what you are trying to achieve.

The trouble with deciding whether you're solving the right

to keep hiding and not to find another thing to hide it behind, but to realise that we don't need to hide in the first place — that we're okay as we are, that we are unconditionally human.

There is no simple recipe or checklist for connecting with that deep sense inside you that tells you that you're okay as you are. Some people are lucky enough to live from a place of feeling fundamentally loved and accepted and see others in the same way. Many, maybe most, carry parts of ourselves that forget our unconditional humanity.

I suspect that founders are particularly overrepresented in this group because we are often driven to build and achieve by some chip on our shoulder, looking to prove to someone, real or imaginary, that we deserve to be loved and accepted. Eventually, we realise that we can't prove it and that no proof was ever required in the first place. Only once we drop this weight do we realise how much we might have carried our entire lives.

WHAT IF I HAVE NOTHING TO DO?

The fear of an empty calendar may sound unusual or even unreasonable. After all, aren't we founding startups precisely so that we could be in charge of our time and, after selling the business, have the freedom to do or not do anything at all?

I'm thinking of one founder who, having built a successful business and announced to his team that he's stepping down as a CEO (but staying around as a founder without a clear job spec), found himself as busy as he used to be, getting pulled into different areas of the business. It wasn't until he saw that his diary hadn't changed much since "stepping down" that he realised that whatever his intentions, he hadn't made a meaningful change.

Facing the empty calendar was scary for him. For years, he was optimising every hour of his day, doing more work, meeting more people, solving problems and being busy. Yet, a part of him knew that something had to change.

What emerged for him as he consciously started to create space in his life was the fear of being irrelevant, of becoming the kind of person wasting days in leisure without enjoying it. In reality, once he summoned the courage to slow down and be less busy, what emerged was a long-repressed drive to focus on his personal development.

For over a decade, the only thing that mattered to him was the business's performance. His effort was rewarded with a profitable company employing hundreds of people nationwide, but it might have masked more profound questions. Who am I when I'm not running the business? What are my interests and passions? What is my life calling me to do?

An empty calendar can be terrifying because a part inside us knows that there are essential questions we aren't answering when running too fast. We don't know what we'll discover when we slow down. What if there are more fears there? What if it's overwhelming?

If we face the questions that come up when we aren't distracting ourselves with work or leisure, we inevitably find out that we have what it takes to confront them. We also see that confronting them leads to deeper self-awareness and personal growth.

My invitation to any founder who fears that they'll step down and won't know what to do with their days is to treat this as an exceptional opportunity to discover what they need to face. It might be that the fear of an empty calendar is coming up for those founders who sense that how they've been living their life up until now isn't working anymore, and they are called to do some inner work. Uncertainty tends to be uncomfortable but abundant with lessons about where we are still stuck and what we need to work on.

In my experience, and in the experience of many other founders I know, it's usually a mistake to jump straight into something else right after stepping down as a CEO. However tempting a new business idea can be, and however uncomfortable the feeling of not having the usual meetings on the calendar can be, taking time to slow down and process the change that has just happened can be invaluable.

As entrepreneurs, we are excited about new beginnings, ideas, and opportunities. However, we tend to be less adept with endings. Yet, they are just as crucial for something new to emerge. Even when we are sure that stepping down as a CEO is right, there are parts of the job that we will be missing and parts of our identity that we are shedding. Honouring this transition and grieving all the good bits that we're leaving behind can help us put it to rest and focus on the road ahead.

WHAT IF I AM UNEMPLOYABLE?

Another big fear many founders have is that they will be unemployable. This is usually shared as a joke: "I have been working for myself for so long, no one will ever hire me," but it has both a grain of truth and a grain of fear.

The grain of truth is that startup founders are in a weird spot regarding employability. On the one hand, they have valuable qualities and skills: management and sales experience, resilience, tenacity, business acumen, resourcefulness and many others. On the other hand, they usually aren't professional CEOs with a track record of taking over someone else's company and taking it to the next level. Starting a business and taking over someone else's business to lead are two very different jobs.

When it comes to C-level roles, founder CEOs often need greater skills in that particular area. As founder CEOs, our roles are inevitably broad. Even if we excelled in a functional area – CTO, CFO, CPO – before stepping up to become a CEO, the transition to becoming someone else's C-level executive is rarely straightforward.

This creates a paradoxical situation in which the founder CEO may be the perfect person for their job at their company, but the path to the next step in their career may be less obvious.

The grain of fear in this is, nonetheless, misguided. As we will see in the last chapter, there are several career paths that founder CEOs who stepped down tend to follow, and I've yet to come across an example of a founder CEO unable to figure out what's next for them. It may take time or effort, but if you have what it takes to build a startup, you have what it takes to land on your feet after leaving it.

The way to approach this fear is to acknowledge that it is true that we, as founders, have many excellent and valuable skills, and it's equally true that we may need to learn how to present our gifts to the world. We spent years learning to sell our vision at every opportunity: to new hires, future investors, the board and the media. We can undoubtedly learn to sell our skills to the market if needed. We'll discuss how other founders do it in the final chapter.

WHAT WILL MY INVESTORS THINK OF ME?

Another fear is letting down your investors. Contrary to a stereotype according to which it's easy for startup founders to be spending someone else's money building their unicorns, most founders I know have a deep sense of responsibility towards the investors they raised from and respect for the faith their investors put in them. Like founders, venture capitalists raise money from their investors and are under as much pressure to deliver impressive results as the founders themselves.

This respect is healthy. It's only right to treat someone else's cash as your own (or better!). The desire to do the right thing by delivering a great exit first and the fear of initiating a difficult conversation sometimes stops founders from the discomfort of telling their investors that they are considering or have decided to step down.

This can be misguided. First, professional venture capitalists are grown-ups who account for the risk of a founder stepping down and, therefore, price it in by offering terms that take this risk into account.

One founder, as he was raising his next round nine years after he started his business, was asked by the investors whether he might be considering stepping down. As experienced operators, they knew what running a startup for a decade is like. He sincerely said he was as committed as ever, but a few months later, he realised he needed to step down. His investors happened to see what he might not have yet seen himself.

Secondly, and just as importantly, stepping down might be in the investors' interests. If another CEO takes over with new ideas and energy, it may increase the chances of the company delivering a great return on investment. Therefore, it would be misguided for founders to avoid stepping down out of obligation to stay until an exit.

Finally, the investors won't necessarily see stepping down as a problem. Rory Stirling, a general partner at Connect Ventures, fully respects the right of the CEO to choose to step down, as long as it's done responsibly:

> "A CEO can leave when they decide they want to leave. Ultimately, they're a human being with complete autonomy over whether they want to continue in a role or not. There are three scenarios where it's appropriate to step down.
>
> The first scenario, they believe they are no longer the best person for the job. The second is when they are burnt out or can't continue without risking their own physical or mental health.
>
> And then there is a third one that surprised me, but it's true, which is when they can no longer afford to continue. You can imagine a scenario where a company can't afford to pay the CEO what they need to be paid. Frankly, I think that's also a viable reason if, for a period of time, they might just be risking their own or their family's well-being.
>
> However, what could be inappropriate is stepping down to get a better-paid job somewhere else. I think that's a terrible reason. That feels completely inappropriate to me. We've invested, we've formed trust in backing this company. Of course, that depends on the distance from the funding round, right? This could be five years on, in which case, it's entirely appropriate as things change. But if it's months on, then it feels entirely inappropriate."

Our job as CEOs is not to last in our seats for as long as we can. Our job is to make the business successful. If replacing ourselves with another CEO will likely make the business more successful, the right thing to do is to discuss it with the board. Feelings of guilt that may accompany this conversation are natural and understandable, but they aren't a reason to stay in a job we should otherwise leave.

WHAT IF I WON'T BE ABLE TO RAISE AGAIN?

A related fear is that stepping down will prevent founders from raising money again. One founder, reflecting on her stepping down as a CEO, said:

> "I was scared of people's judgement. Of course, I was. When I did end up publishing on LinkedIn that I was leaving, I got a lot of positive comments. But I also discovered that VCs all want to know why I quit. Because as a founder, you're supposed to either take it to exit or to death. And to resign is suspicious. What was the reason there?"

What matters is how it's done, not whether you ever left your position as a founder CEO. If the business was handed over to a new CEO, who took it to new heights, congratulations! It's a mark of success to take the business to the point when it's ready for the next growth stage under a new leader, not a failure.

It's a far better outcome for the business and your reputation than trying to take the company to the next level while you are exhausted or lack the skills for that growth stage. If the business fails or struggles, you won't get a medal for not leaving earlier.

Nic Brisbourne, CEO at Forward Partners, agrees that what matters is how the founder behaved, not whether they chose to leave:

> "If you're seen to cut and run too quickly, that can be a

> problem because potential future investors will fear that if things ever go sideways, you will be gone in a second. Conversely, as long as everyone can see you gave it your all and handled the transition well, leaving prior to exit won't impact your ability to raise for your next company."

The way to address this fear is to remember that your ability to raise money depends on two things: the results you deliver and how you face difficulties. If you work hard as a founder, show self-awareness, treat others with respect, face challenges head-on, welcome difficult conversations and behave with integrity, that's what will influence your chances of raising again, not how long you managed to stay in your job past the point when it made sense to do so.

HOW WILL I PAY MY BILLS?

Another fear that occasionally stops founder CEOs from considering stepping down is not knowing how to cover their expenses while navigating this transition. Contrary to a stereotype held by those who never started a business, founders aren't always flush with cash, particularly those who haven't had a big exit before.

Your company may be doing well, and your salary may be comfortable, but that's different from being able to afford to go unpaid for several months or more while you figure out what to do next, especially if you have a family to support.

This is a very practical concern. As I will argue later in the book, it's pragmatic for a business to give the outgoing founder financial certainty, as this will make the transition easier and increase the chances of success.

It certainly makes sense to start this conversation with the board.

They may be very open to giving you financial certainty for practical reasons, but it's unlikely to be on top of their concerns unless you raise it yourself.

However, the business won't always be able to do it. In this case, trying to find your next job (or a way to lower expenses) may make sense before you commit to stepping down. Yet, financial concerns aren't a good enough reason to stay for long in a CEO job that you would otherwise leave. Instead, it's an invitation to create a transition plan, taking the reality of your financial situation and obligations into account and then making it happen.

Somewhat paradoxically, some founders can be great at managing company money but hopeless at managing their personal finances. In the office, we create detailed forecasts, carefully thinking about gross margins and cost structures, but at home, we spend what we have in the current account without thinking much about it. If this sounds like you, a great way to face this fear could be talking to someone you trust who'll listen non-judgementally and help you make sense of your situation.

WHAT IF THE NEW CEO SCREWS UP?

If you're the only person who ever ran your business, it can be hard to imagine that someone else could do your job, let alone do it far better than you. It could be easier to imagine worst-case scenarios of the new CEO failing your business.

A slightly related fear is that the new CEO will make the company financially successful but will sacrifice its culture or violate its values, ruining what you worked so hard to build.

It can be helpful to remember that the job of the new CEO is not to replace you like-for-like. Their job is to be a great CEO. They will likely make different decisions, be guided by different principles, and take the company in a different direction. Yet none of that by itself means that they'll be doing a bad job.

The way to approach this fear is to consider whether you haven't found the right candidate yet or if you're assuming you'll never find someone you can trust. If you're having doubts about a specific person you're considering your successor, it's worth going deep into these concerns. You'll never have perfect certainty that they're the best person, but you should be certain enough.

Like any other hire, you want to be excited about them taking the job. Would you hire a CTO if you doubted their ability to lead the tech function? Would you hire a sales executive if you didn't believe in their ability to sell? A new CEO is no different. Set the bar high, and don't compromise.

However, it may be the case that you struggle to imagine anyone possibly taking the top role and doing a great job. In this case, looking inside and working with your own fear is the way to approach it.

What is it exactly that you're afraid of? How does it feel in the body? Can you stay with it? Can you relax into it? What happens if you write those fears down on a piece of paper? What if you explain it to a trusted friend, coach or therapist who will listen and help you make sense of the fear?

A new CEO may indeed fail at their job, but it's not a reason to never trust anyone.

WHAT IF MY SUCCESSOR SMASHES IT?

This fear is counterintuitive. Flavia, a founder in transition, captures it this way:

> "So you know, all this work we've done to get ready

> to be this amazingly successful business? And then the new guy takes over, and this thing flies! Suddenly, he's a superstar? And I'm like, fuck, I can't do that."

That's how our ego can set us up for failure by putting us in a double bind. The ego says, "If I hire the wrong CEO and they ruin the company, I'll feel like I failed. Either I failed at hiring, or the company was not strong enough — it doesn't matter; it'll be my failure to reckon with."

And, the ego continues: "What does it say about me if I hire the right CEO and the company becomes vastly more successful? I couldn't have done it myself? I left at the wrong time? Was I the problem to begin with?"

Sometimes, we are afraid of our own success. As with all fears, it's critical to see the fear for what it is: just a series of thoughts and sensations in the body (fear never feels nice or is just a thought; our embodied experience is what makes this emotion feel like fear).

A much more helpful perspective is to remember two things. One is that the success of the new CEO is precisely what you aim for if you're leaving. There might be a part of you that feels a bit insecure about that, and it's okay to have it. We can notice this insecurity and let it be, simply noticing it as a pattern of thoughts and feelings.

The other thing to remember is that the business's success doesn't define our success in life or our worth. We can have more or less money in our bank account, and our company can be incredibly successful or fail to take off — none of that says anything about our inherent worth as human beings. You don't become a better person when you IPO your business at the stock exchange, and you don't become a worse person when you call in the administrators.

No one who has deeply reflected on what really matters to them in life — and what defines them as a human being — has concluded it to be the success of their business. If they have, they haven't thought deeply enough.

As we discussed at the beginning of the chapter, the goal is not to banish or ignore our fears. If we try to do that, they will find a way to sabotage our lives. Instead, we need to get to know them, listen to them, and see what they have to say and what they are trying to teach us. We must treat them with respect and even gratitude because each fear is trying to protect us from something.

Paradoxically, the more you work with your fears, the more of them you might discover, but they will feel less scary as you grow in your confidence to face each of them.

Now, once we have spent some time reflecting on our inner world, let's turn our attention to the practical circumstances of our lives in the next chapter. Your skill set, your company's needs, your board position, and your family — all of these will influence if and how you choose to step down.

Questions to reflect on:

- What insights do my fears offer about my deepest values and priorities?
- Which of my fears feels most paralysing, and why does it hold such power over me?
- How do my fears influence my decision-making, and what patterns can I identify?
- How can I create a support system or community that empowers me to embrace and work through my fears?
- How can I cultivate a mindset that reinforces my resilience and capability in the face of adversity?

CHAPTER 3

ASSESS YOUR SITUATION

You must consider your practical circumstances to decide between stepping down as a CEO and staying. However, we inevitably see our circumstances through the prism of our minds, so it is necessary to start with the most profound questions: who you are, what you are meant to be doing, and what your fears are. All these questions are subjective: they are about you, your heart, and your soul.

In this chapter, we'll aim to understand your situation more objectively. What is your skill set? Most importantly, are you more of a founder or more of a CEO? Which of them does your business need right now? How sound are your personal finances? How does your board see your performance? Who's there to support you on this journey?

Working through these questions will inform your next steps: whether you decide to step down and, if so, how you kick this process off, as we'll discuss in the chapter that follows.

ARE YOU A FOUNDER OR A CEO?

When I assumed the title of the CEO of a startup of ten people, I wasn't really a CEO. I was a founder. A founder's job is to ensure the company doesn't crash on takeoff and finds initial product-market fit. To do this, the founder focuses on three big things: talking to customers, hiring the early team and building the product, among many other tasks. The founder is involved in every aspect of the business and ensures that the product solves a meaningful problem for the customer.

The job of a CEO is to build and run the company that makes the product that solves the customer's problem. The CEO sets the vision, builds the team, and ensures that they have the cash and clarity to succeed.

Jeff Lynn, founder and first CEO of Seedrs, an equity crowdfunding company in the UK, who hired his replacement a few years in, described the difference:

> "When you start a brand new business, particularly in an innovative space, you need to be a little bit crazy, a little bit willing to take a lot of chances to see what works, and a lot of flexibility and agility to tackle things as they are thrown at you. Whereas leading a business as it grows requires a much more planned, thoughtful, disciplined approach to leadership. There are a few people out there who are able to do both, but in my mind, they are very different personality types and skills."

This shift from building the product to building the company that is making the product is usually gradual and subtle. At this point, the founder must step into the role of CEO, even if they have held the title for years.

This shift often begins when the business is around the Series A investment stage or an equivalent set of metrics for bootstrapped companies. Simply put, there is a product, some good traction, a team of a few dozen people and a sense that the company has validated its riskiest assumptions and is ready to grow.

At this point, founders often make the mistake of doubling down on what got them to the Series A stage, aiming to get to the Series B (or equivalent for bootstrapped businesses). However, what got you here won't get you there. Counterintuitively, the behaviours that helped the founder take the business to Series A will now get in the way.

To get to Series A, the founder was likely managing by intuition, without a robust set of metrics to guide them. They were directly involved in every aspect of the business. They probably didn't have strong enough support in some areas like finance or HR; instead, they focused on product and technology. They almost certainly led sales personally without a repeatable and documented process.

However, doubling down on these behaviours will likely make the situation worse. What will help the company get to Series B will be focusing on building the company that makes the product, having clear metrics for different aspects of the business, having a repeatable and scalable sales process, and professional support across all business areas.

This is when a founder starts to change how they lead, taking their seat as a CEO. From the founder's perspective, this looks like a transition from founder to CEO. The same process looks like Series A to Series B growth from a venture capitalist's perspective. At this point, founders often question how long they want to keep running the business.

It's worth thinking proactively about whether and when to step down without waiting until you have to because the more time the founder and the board have to address the question, the more room for manoeuvre they have.

Let's look at the situation of a founder stepping down before, during or after the transition from founder to CEO.

Before the transition, the reasons for stepping down tend to be related to pressure or performance. After years of trying to find product-market fit and build the right team while managing the runway, it's easy to feel exhausted or question whether this particular opportunity is worth the effort.

Performance may also be an issue. Sometimes, despite the best efforts and the willingness to continue, it becomes clear to the board and the founder that they don't have what it takes to make this business successful.

During the transition to taking the seat as a CEO, an additional risk is that this is different from what the founder is looking for. One of my clients compared being a founder to riding a jet ski, making sharp turns and enjoying the speed. To him, being the CEO of a larger business felt like being the captain of a large boat manned by dozens of people. Not every jet ski rider wants to be a captain. Some want to keep riding the jet ski.

Long after the transition, a founder may find themselves bored once the business is steady and successful. Sure, they can grow the business and expand to another country, but what's the point? When was the last time they took a long vacation with their kids? What matters in life? Asking big questions may well lead to a re-evaluation of priorities. Choosing a new CEO with the energy and vision to run the business for the next decade can be a wise move.

In reality, it's rarely this simple. Founders can feel both burnt out and bored, productive and overwhelmed, clear and confused – often on the same day. However, once the idea of stepping down comes to mind, it doesn't always go away. To prevent it from being an ongoing distraction, founders need a way to think about this question to be clear when they're still committed and when it's time to go. Constantly looking at the door without leaving doesn't serve anyone.

If you're in, you're in. If you're not, you don't have to be. But don't sit on the fence. As we'll explore later in the book, not making a decision serves neither you nor the company.

One of the questions to ask yourself is how your skillset and ambition align with the business's needs at this stage. There's no right or wrong answer here. Some founders conclude that they are a "founder, not a CEO", better at starting companies than operating them. Others can't wait to leave the messy early founding stages behind so that they can do their best work as CEOs.

Reflecting on the differences between the skillset of a founder and that of a CEO, as well as the demands from the business as it keeps growing, will influence how you'll see all other choices you'll have to make during this transition, especially the choice of the successor.

HOW GOOD ARE YOU AT YOUR JOB?

There's no single, straightforward way of evaluating startup CEOs due to the job's complexity and wild differences in the circumstances of different startups. Yet it's indispensable to have a clear sense of how you're doing as a CEO, as this will inform your CEO succession journey.

A good place to start is the job spec. What is yours? The best framework I've seen comes from Fred Wilson, a VC. The CEO has only three jobs: hold the vision, build the team and give them resources to win.

So, let's go through them one by one. How well do you set and hold the vision? How clear is the strategy? You get a sense of your ability to hold the vision by seeing how aligned and clear everyone around you is about why your company exists, what it is meant to do and how it will do it. Most importantly, your team, but also the board, customers, and press — everyone needs to be aligned on why, what and how. This is your job, and if too many people say they don't understand why, what and how, that reflects your skills.

What about your team? Did you attract the best people? Are they working like a well-oiled machine together, or is there constant drama? Are you setting the bar high and managing performance well? Can you trust them to get the job done on time, every time? A sign that you are doing a great job in this area is that most of your focus is on vision, strategy and resources because you know your team is not a limiting factor for your startup.

Does your team have the resources to implement the vision? Usually, this is cash, which is why fundraising and resource allocation are critical responsibilities of a CEO. A team won't achieve much if the business can't pay the bills.

However, these three areas only describe the activities of the startup CEO. What about the outcomes? Is the business under your leadership performing well against properly defined objectives? If your business can translate its vision and resources into appropriate goals and then achieve them, quarter after quarter, year after year, you're likely doing a great job as a CEO.

Taking a view on your performance as a CEO will shape your entire succession journey, from deciding to step down to choosing a successor, negotiating with the board and choosing your next steps. The more clarity you have on your own performance, the more clarity you'll have on the rest of your CEO succession process.

HOW DOES THE BOARD SEE YOUR PERFORMANCE?

Without a doubt, your board has a perspective on your performance. Given that they are on the board so that they could fire you if needed, they are, individually and collectively, somewhere on the spectrum from "the CEO is great" to "the CEO needs to be fired urgently".

If you are being asked to leave in no uncertain terms, you probably need to read a book on negotiations instead (I hope you return to this one when it's all over). But in most cases, the board is either happy with the CEO or willing to give them a chance to grow because firing a CEO is a last resort due to its risks, especially before solid product-market fit.

Understanding how the board sees your performance is essential because it will impact your approach to your own succession. First of all, if you have reasons to suspect the board might be considering letting you go, this can be an argument to take charge of the process yourself. As we'll discuss later, making the first move here can be advantageous.

Second, the better the board's opinion of your performance, the stronger your negotiating position and the more input you'll have into the process, even if you're not the only decision-maker. For example, you'll likely have more influence over who your successor will be, even if it is the entire board's responsibility to appoint them.

If you misjudge the situation by assuming that the board has a poor view of your performance when that's not the case, it can prompt you to make suboptimal decisions, such as stepping down when it would make more sense to stay.

The trouble is that boards can be hard to read. Board members have every incentive to proclaim full and unconditional support of the CEO until they decide to fire them. This is because telling a CEO they're doing a bad job to the point of risking being fired will likely make it more challenging to work together without any obvious upside.

This can also have legal implications. If the CEO resigns and then takes things to court, an employment tribunal can interpret it as constructive dismissal (pushing someone to leave without firing them). This will be painful, distracting and expensive, so startup boards usually avoid this scenario at all costs by giving the impression that the CEO is doing alright until the end.

If you find yourself in a potential constructive dismissal situation where you feel like you have no choice but to leave because of how the board is acting towards you, immediately contact an employment lawyer.

However, things rarely get this bad. If your working relationship with the board is good, you can gauge their sentiments by doing a few things. One is talking to the board about your performance in terms of company performance instead of yourself. Think about all the questions from the previous section. If you sit down with your investors individually and ask them to share their thoughts on how aligned the team is around the vision and strategy, how good the team is, etc., you'll get the data you need to draw conclusions.

If your lead investor says that the vision is muddy, the strategy confusing, the team is second-class, and they've been wondering why the company missed its budget again, but they have full trust in your ability to solve all of this very quickly, don't get complacent. That was an assessment of you as the CEO, not the business.

You can also run a 360 review process, engaging an executive coaching firm to interview every board member about the CEO's performance individually. Having a trained and objective intermediary to debrief 360 review findings provides additional perspective.

Finally, these conversations must happen regularly, starting when the board is formed, not just when you're considering stepping down. You can strengthen your relationship with the board and better understand how they perceive you and the business by regularly discussing your and the company's performance.

ARE YOU A CO-CEO OR A CXO?

Not every company has just one CEO. Additionally, in some cases, the founder holding the CEO's title isn't actually doing the CEO's job. In such scenarios, the process of CEO succession tends to be simpler.

Some startups are run by two co-CEOs, nearly always two co-founders. While this structure does work for some, I've never seen a startup with one CEO that would be better served by two co-CEOs instead. In many, but not all, cases, this structure betrays the fact that the two co-founders never had a conversation about who's really in charge and what each of them is responsible for.

To work well together, two co-CEOs must have similar values

and vision but have complementary skill sets. Furthermore, as the business grows, the co-CEOs must keep growing at roughly the same rate.

While it may look similar to a CEO leaving the business, the dynamics of a co-CEO stepping down tend to be different and easier to navigate. For a start, there's usually the other co-CEO who remains the only CEO, ensuring the continuity of leadership.

Also, the co-CEO who's stepping down can often find a role on the senior team of their startup that would better suit their skill-set if they don't want to leave the business.

So, one of co-CEOs stepping down is not so much a change of leadership but a clarification of where power lies and what skills everyone brings to the table.

A similar dynamic can be seen in founding teams that haven't thought carefully about which founder should have which title according to their skills and ambitions. There, a founder with a CxO title might be doing most of the work of the CEO (fundraising, holding the vision, hiring, and managing the senior team). In contrast, the founder with the CEO title might be doing either a small part of the job or even some other job (e.g. operations or product). They have the title but aren't doing the CEO's job.

Like with co-CEOs, the next step here is to have an honest and open conversation about everyone's skills and ambitions to understand the titles most appropriate for each founder. The earlier this conversation happens, the easier it tends to be for everyone.

HOW STRESSED ARE YOU?

Running a startup is a stressful job. Trying to decide whether to step down as CEO only makes it more difficult. When speaking to CEOs considering stepping down, their well-being comes up in nearly every conversation.

As founders, we tend not to prioritise our own well-being high enough, putting the needs of others and the business first. At times, this might be appropriate, but the risk many founders seem to be blind to is the deterioration of the quality of decision-making.

One word that comes up repeatedly in conversations with founder CEOs is "trapped". I certainly felt this way myself. Flavia, a founder of a successful startup in London, captured the sentiment of many founders when she spoke about her experience:

> "Covid business disruption really took a toll on my mental health. Anyone who's got a job can just leave their job and get another one. When it's your business or you're the CEO, you just can't do that. And it makes you feel trapped."

Angela, a founder CEO who stepped down seven years into running her startup because she was concerned about the toll the emotional intensity of running a startup was taking on her health, later recalled:

> "You do feel quite trapped because it is your baby. You started it, and you love your baby because it's your baby. But at some point, the baby becomes sick. When it's not going so well. On the one hand, you really want to do everything you can, right? But on the other hand, at some point, you start to feel like this is making you sick.
>
> I felt I'd done everything I could to help, but I had to

> walk away because it was physically killing me. And, of course, if you imagine that, you also understand how painful it is to walk away because it's your child."

When we're under significant pressure, we aren't always thinking clearly. Sometimes it is hard to avoid, for example, during the pressure of a fundraise. However, the decision whether to step down or not as a founder CEO ideally shouldn't be taken when we feel like we ran out of options and don't believe in our business anymore.

This isn't simply about feeling good. Well-being matters, but what also matters is the quality of our decisions. Choosing to step down as a CEO will have significant consequences both for the company and the founder. Whenever possible, it should be approached with due care and attention. The stakes are too high.

If at all possible, a founder CEO feeling like they're on the cusp of making this decision would be well-advised to take a break, possibly go away to forget about the distraction of running the business day-to-day and reflect, either in solitude or in the company of trusted and wise people who are thoroughly familiar with the situation.

My good friend Noah Abelson-Gertler, a founder and CEO of a public company, dreamed for years of leaving the business. One day, feeling burnt out, he woke up with the realisation that he had to leave for the sake of his own well-being. At that time, he and his wife were preparing to start a family. For him, the prospect of being a present father was far more important than his role as a CEO of a public company.

Recalling, years later, the drama that ensued when the shareholders started to fight bitterly behind each other's backs for company control as he felt flat-out exhausted, he wished he had started preparing much earlier and much more seriously for the transition, learning from the experience of others who had done it before instead of leaving it until the point when he felt he couldn't do it anymore.

From my own personal experience, it felt like a luxury to take a lot of time off to make one decision, but given how consequential it is, it is worth taking it very seriously. Some of my best moments of reflection occurred when I was hiking alone in the forests around Chamonix in the French Alps, riding my motorcycle around Scotland or Switzerland, or attending meditation retreats.

Being in nature, ideally with the phone switched off to minimise distractions, can bring clarity that can be elusive when we're overwhelmed with emails and Slack messages.

CAN YOU AFFORD TO STEP DOWN?

One of the practical questions you'll need to reflect on when considering a founder transition is your financial situation.

While entrepreneurship may be glamorised in the media, founders don't always have significant savings to fall back on after leaving the business. Furthermore, founders tend to be paid below market for a very long time because of the pressure from investors who really should know better and because of their own judgment, often misguided, that the startup needs money more than them.

I remember speaking to a founder who was very stressed because of his financial situation, living paycheque to paycheque and not being able to afford a holiday. He was paying himself £30,000/year, admitting he didn't feel he "deserved" to be paid more until the business was more successful.

At that point, the business was turning over a million in revenue a year and had raised money. Doubling the salary would have been a great investment for the startup: it would be run by a founder whose full focus would be on the business, not on his bank balance.

Financial considerations may significantly influence the decision to leave or its timing, leading to a suboptimal outcome for all parties involved: the company, the investors and the founder themselves. Without consciously acknowledging it, a founder may procrastinate on doing what's right because they must keep paying the mortgage. This is unfortunate because the amount of money in question is often insignificant for the business, but the costs for the company can be very real.

A CEO who isn't going to do a great job because they burned out or lost interest in running the business but isn't actively preparing for the CEO transition is doing the business and the team a disservice by not ensuring that the startup has a great leader in place. If financial uncertainty stops the founder from taking action, that's a lose-lose situation for everyone involved.

This is why I advocate for startup boards to be generous towards CEOs stepping down. Not out of compassion (don't we all have bills to pay?), but out of a pragmatic understanding that the CEO should be able to make the best decisions for the business without undue worries about their own financial situation.

Thankfully, some investors agree. Rory Stirling stresses the importance of supporting the founders' well-being, including their financial position. He recalled one CEO telling him he needed to step down.

> "First and foremost, the most important thing was that we had a CEO come to us and say that he needed to step

> down for personal health reasons. You've just got to make that happen and make sure that he's safe and well, which, by the way, may also include making sure that he doesn't suddenly have financial insecurity. Nothing will be worse than having a breakdown at the same point as losing your job and losing your income."

It saddens me that some investors seem to take the opposite approach: to keep the founder financially locked in until the big exit, presumably out of fear that otherwise, they'd jump ship when the going gets tough.

This is misguided. Great companies aren't built by indentured labour. They are built by people who want to make it happen so much that they keep working through thick and thin for years, regardless of the challenges coming their way. Suppose a founder believes, for whatever reason, that they shouldn't be running the startup anymore. In that case, I can't see how obstructing their exit leads to a healthy culture and a successful business.

This is a tricky situation because writing "golden parachute" clauses into founder employment contracts might not be appropriate either, not least because the right thing to do depends on the startup's financial situation and other factors. However, the board and the founders should, ideally, have built enough trust for the outgoing CEO to know that they are financially safe to choose to hand over to someone else if it's the right thing to do.

Another concern many founders face is the fear that they are unemployable, as we discussed earlier and will return to later in the book. While everyone eventually lands on their feet because, as entrepreneurs, we are a tenacious and resourceful bunch, it might take more time than for other people who are used to going from a job in one company to a similar job in another.

It's also true to say that outgoing founders have a deep need to rest. Running a startup is stressful in ways only people who choose to launch their own thing can understand. Often, although not always, a startup CEO leaves their job at some stage of burnout, looking to slow down and recover instead of jumping into another job.

I remember telling my coach, as we discussed my stepping down, that if I left only to start looking for a job at another company because of financial pressure, I might as well stay. Even though that looked like a rational position to me then, I was thinking short-term, ultimately putting both myself and my company in a lose-lose situation. As I'll keep repeating, it's okay to stay, and it's okay to leave, but don't sit on the fence. It doesn't serve anyone.

So, my invitation to both founders and boards of directors is to be open to the conversation about the founder's financial situation in case they need to leave the business. For founders, this means being comfortable with raising this question with other decision-makers without the fear of appearing greedy. For boards, this means being pragmatic and ensuring that founders have the financial freedom to focus on what's best for the company long-term, including the change in leadership.

HOW WILL THE TRANSITION IMPACT YOUR FAMILY?

Every founder in transition with children will think about how their decision to keep running the business or step down will affect their family. We spend a lot of time in the office, but every parent knows that their family comes before business.

We can't make significant business decisions, including whether to step down as a CEO, without considering what it means for our families. Some founders find ways to combine parenthood with the intensity of running a business. Others don't. As one CEO in transition, Frances, said:

> "I don't want us never to see our kids because we work such long hours. This wouldn't be a great life for me. And I'd seen female founders do things like send investor updates from the hotel or the hospital room when they were having contractions or go back to work six weeks after their babies were born. And I thought, Fucking kudos to you! That's incredible! But if I were to become a mom, I don't think that's how I want to do it."

This sentiment was echoed by another founder, Flavia:

> "I've got two little kids. Well, they're not that little anymore. They're only a few years away from not really wanting me around as much. I had two weeks of maternity leave with my first child, and I only took three months with the second one. So, for their entire life, their mom has not been the primary giver; that's been my husband. I don't want to look back when I am 55, and I'm mega-wealthy and mega-successful, feeling like I missed their childhood. I'm at a phase in my life where my personal successes are not as important as my family anymore."

There isn't a single right answer here. There are brilliant examples of parents who combine high-pressure jobs with the demands of parenthood and brilliant examples of parents who choose to spend more time with their family, even if it means leaving a high-pressure job. It's a personal decision all parents have to make.

However, it goes without saying that if a CEO wants to start a family and continue in their role but feels that the company or the board isn't willing to make reasonable accommodations to make that possible, that's probably discrimination. I wouldn't be touching on this subject if it wasn't so common. Unfortunately, it sometimes leads to founder CEOs leaving the business they should otherwise still be running.

In one particularly egregious recent case in the UK, the board of directors singled out the founder CEO as the only person who wouldn't be included in the next round of options grants upon learning that she was pregnant. This is illegal and immoral; sadly, this is only one example out of several.

This founder chose to engage an employment lawyer and stand her ground. While her story is far from over as of this writing, I'm optimistic that law and common sense will prevail. Being bullied by your board members who are expected to be by your side is not a reason to leave your job as a CEO. If you find yourself in this situation, please remember that you are not alone and reach out to employment lawyers, other entrepreneurs or those you respect in the tech industry to help you plan your next steps.

WHO IS IN YOUR TRUSTED CIRCLE OF SUPPORTERS?

Deciding to step down as a CEO is a big decision that shouldn't be taken alone. In my case, I relied on many close supporters who listened to me, challenged my thinking, offered different perspectives and ultimately helped me chart a path forward. I'm incredibly grateful for not going through this journey alone. Whoever your trusted circle of supporters are, lean on them, listen to them and stress-test your decisions with them.

My family, who know me better than many, was trying to alert me to signs of living in an unsustainable way for years. Out of countless conversations, I remember a phone call with my sister, who caught me in a moment of feeling particularly low and asked me how long I would keep working like this.

Founder friends, some of whom left the companies they founded and others still running them, helped me normalise how I was feeling and put my own experiences and struggles into perspective. What is normal if you're a founder? What is too much? How do others really feel when they aren't taking gorgeous selfies for their LinkedIn feeds to show how they're killing it? You find out in late-night conversations over a glass of wine.

My coaches — I worked with five of them over the years of being a CEO — helped me see the bigger picture whenever I felt lost in the drama of the moment. When it's so tempting to focus on how we feel right now, what happened this week, and our bank account today, we need to take a big step back, and then another one, to really see the perspective because a decision to step down as a CEO will have long-lasting consequences. My coaches helped me do that. They also helped me understand why I felt the way I did, see the narratives in my mind more clearly and find more compassion for myself.

A therapist helped me to work through the feelings with infinite patience. Having left a high-pressure sales leadership role many years ago to become a therapist and mindfulness teacher, he helped me learn to be present to my experience without reacting to it.

My psychiatrist was there for me when I was at my lowest point to reassure me that it was not as bad as it felt at the moment and to help me find mental clarity.

Lucy, an executive coach and a friend, inspired me to enter the coaching profession. Her grounding presence helped me navigate the transition.

My friend and co-founder Rob, who chose to step down as a CEO himself years before me and since then invested in and mentored dozens of founders at Techstars as the MD of their Berlin programme, was there for me any time I needed to speak to someone who would always understand.

Finally, my board of directors has been as supportive as I could only hope, which is one of the main reasons we all look back at the CEO succession and feel it went very well. Their pragmatism and support made all the difference in helping the business and me to navigate the transition.

Whoever your trusted circle of supporters are, don't feel you must make this decision alone. No one will be able to make it for you, but hearing different perspectives and feeling the support of others will bring clarity and confidence.

As a founder considering stepping down, you must clearly understand your situation. Perhaps one of the most critical questions is whether your skill set lies in being a founder or a CEO and what skill set the business needs at this point. This, together with a reflection on how well you are doing your job, will give you a richer perspective.

This will also help you take a stance if your board suggests you leave or if you suspect it might do so soon. This will affect how the CEO succession will proceed if it goes ahead.

Reflecting on your skills, company needs, board position, finances, and stress levels will help guide your CEO transition with trusted supporters.

All the work you've done up until now, reflecting on your circumstances, fears, dreams and hopes, has led you to the big question we will address in the next chapter. Should you step down as a CEO?

Questions to reflect on:

- In what ways do my strengths align or diverge from what's required of me as a CEO?
- How can I objectively assess my performance as a CEO?
- Who are potential allies, mentors, or coaches who can guide me through my CEO transition?
- What practices or environments can foster the solitude and clarity I need for deep reflection?
- What are my non-negotiables in balancing personal well-being with professional ambition?

CHAPTER 4

MAKE THE DECISION

Having reflected on your inner and outer worlds, you're in an excellent position to decide whether to step down. This decision shouldn't be rushed, but sitting on the fence wouldn't be right either.

Stepping down isn't a binary choice: to stay as a CEO or to leave. We'll discuss multiple possible options in this chapter, including selling the business, returning money to investors or changing your role.

However, it's not enough to make a decision. Making a decision that will stand the test of time is essential. Was that a good decision if you "decide" to stay as a CEO but start doubting yourself a month later when a crisis hits? Likewise, if you step down as CEO only to realise a few months later that what you needed was a long holiday, that would equally be a mistake.

In this chapter, we'll also talk about strategies to make a decision you are confident in before discussing how and when to kick off the process if you choose to do it.

THE PERILS OF INDECISION

It can be scary to consider whether we should step down even in the privacy of our thoughts. For me, it brought up all my fears and insecurities, so my mind would recoil and distract me by answering a few more emails or scrolling through LinkedIn so that I didn't have to feel discomfort.

Would it mean that I was a failure? I felt trapped between a rock and a hard place. My ego told me I had two options: stay and continue to suffer as a CEO, or quit and feel like a failure for years. I imagined that others would never want to take me seriously, I would never get another job, let alone a CEO of anything, that I would never be able to raise money for another venture and would even be obliged by some unspoken convention to tattoo the word "quitter" on my forearm.

And so, the first mistake I made was procrastinating on it. The problem with indecision was twofold. It was incredibly distracting to have a part of my mind constantly thinking about whether I should step down instead of being focused on the business.

We know, as CEOs, that internal disagreement or weak commitments ruin team performance. Likewise, a major conflict between different parts of ourselves can significantly undermine our well-being.

This indecision made me a worse CEO. Being a good CEO is hard enough if all your attention is on the job. It's much harder if you're not sure if you want the job in the first place.

So, my big mistake was allowing this indecision to linger for about two years instead of addressing it when the doubts first came. The job of a CEO is to identify potential challenges for the business and focus on the most important ones. I didn't prioritise my own indecision as a big enough problem.

It's our responsibility to be aware of our commitment level and act decisively if we find ourselves sitting on the fence, unsure about what we want to do professionally for the next decade.

EXITING AS AN ALTERNATIVE TO STEPPING DOWN

For a founder who doesn't see themselves running their own company anymore, for any reason, the obvious alternative to consider is selling the business. However, this may be difficult to accomplish, or it may go against the interests of other stakeholders — or even the founder CEO themselves.

It would be a mistake to confuse the interests of the founder CEO and the interests of the business in such a situation because the correct timing of selling the business and the right approach to it will rarely align perfectly with the right timing for the founder CEO to leave.

Instead, these two perspectives need to be considered separately. One is all about the founder: what's the right thing for them? The other is about the business: when and how is it right to exit? The overwhelming chances are that the answers will be different.

Startup exits are opportunistic. The best way to sell the company is to build a great business and be open to opportunities. Trying to control the timing or having a CEO who's considering leaving can reduce the strategic options available to the business.

Stepping down as a founder CEO and exiting the business are unlikely to be aligned even if the founder CEO controls the board because their goals and preferences as a human being might not align well with their goals as a shareholder. A human being may feel like the last thing they want to do is to run this company for another year, and they'd accept the first decent offer. The shareholder in them may decide that hiring another

CEO to keep growing the business may lead to a materially better return a few years later.

Therefore, these two questions should not be confused. One is about the person who might be considering leaving their job. Another is about the business, its shareholders and its goals — whether it's maximising enterprise value or social impact. Trying to "solve" both in one go is more likely than not to lead to poor deal terms or the deal falling apart.

There is another practical consideration that may get in the way of selling the business instead of stepping down. In many cases, the acquirer will insist on the continuity of leadership by locking in the founder CEO as an employee for a period of up to a few years, known as an earnout.

While there are examples of founders who find their earnout period happy and relaxing, there seem to be many more who resent the golden handcuffs that shackle them to the otherwise thankless job of integrating their business into a new entity, following someone else's orders. To many, this may seem the opposite of stepping down: you're still locked in, but now you're not even in charge anymore.

Incidentally, one way to avoid the earnout is not to be in the leadership position when the business is sold. While it is never the sole reason to step down, it could be considered a collateral benefit.

One founder of a sizeable UK-based business, who'll remain anonymous, not only appointed an MD to run the company before selling it, but he deliberately acted as the most useless person in interactions with a potential acquirer. It was a high-stakes gamble, but the acquirer concluded that the business was great, except the founder wasn't adding value to it. They offered to buy it without an earnout for the founder. This story is still told in entrepreneurial circles after a few drinks, a decade after the company was sold.

In most cases, it's not easier to exit the business as a way to stop running it. These are two different events happening on different timelines and for different reasons. Forcing them to be aligned is rarely the best move.

BECOMING A GROUP CEO

Leaving the startup CEO's job to focus on something new doesn't always mean leaving the business. Weiting Liu, founder and CEO of Arc.Dev and Codementor, found himself stuck in his role, feeling unable to take the business on a fast-growth trajectory. However, Weiting was equally unwilling to give up on a business that could be profitable if only it weren't spending money on his attempts to find ways to grow.

The turning point for Weiting was recognising that while he set out to build a venture-scale startup, he had a good lifestyle business on his hands: clear product-market fit, loyal customers and healthy unit economics. However, his passion lay in fast-growth startups, not running a small and profitable company. Weiting summed it up in an email to the board:

> "We've been treating a 10-year-old company like a startup, and we keep trying to grow an existing business as if it's still a startup with mixed results."

The way forward for Weiting turned out to be stepping up and becoming the CEO of a group structure that includes the existing business. Instead of trying to make the existing business grow, this structure allowed Weiting to start from scratch and experiment with new ideas.

The "old" business is now run by a new CEO, whom Weiting promoted from a COO position. The new CEO's job is to deliver reliable cash flow instead of trying to make a lifestyle business a fast-growth one.

For Weiting and his team, this is a double win. The core business now focuses on profitability, not growth. For Weiting, it's an opportunity to work on new ideas while having funds to deploy from the existing business. Crucially, this allowed Weiting to stay close to the business and avoid leaving it altogether.

This is a relatively rare move, but it may make sense when the founder has built a company that could be a good, profitable business but wants to work on venture-scale opportunities. Instead of pushing the existing business to grow faster, starting a new one within the existing structure may be easier to give the founder CEO space to focus on building something new.

RETURNING MONEY TO INVESTORS

Jack raised venture capital for his startup from respected London-based investors on the strength of early traction, but then the startup struggled to make further progress. After years of trying, Jack reached a point of being burnt out.

Like so many other founders in such a situation, Jack tried to fix things by taking breaks or swapping responsibilities with his co-founder, but eventually, he chose to step down.

Having agreed with his technical co-founder that he would take over as the CEO, Jack spoke to Rory Stirling, their lead investor on the board. Explaining that he was exhausted and his co-founder was willing to take over, he was hugely relieved to hear the board agree that he should step back immediately.

Rory, reflecting on that conversation with Jack, recalled focusing on empathy for his situation instead of allowing fear to take over:

> "In that moment, I had empathy and I did not react from fear and greed. It's so easy in such a moment to instantly think, 'Shit, this isn't going well, I'm gonna have to explain this to my team next week.'
>
> Instead, I could just see him as a human in front of me who was suffering and be incredibly sympathetic and focused on him. And then, once we've done that, ask the relevant question: For us, as well as for significant shareholders in the company, what does this mean, and what's the right thing to do?"

Knowing that Rory understands where he's coming from, Jack started assessing his options and planning the next steps with their investors.

They found a win-win situation for everyone involved. The investors got 50% of their money back from a bold bet that didn't work out, the founders got a clean cap table without institutional capital on it, and the company kept a bit of cash to allow the new CEO to do another raise or attempt another pivot.

This is unusual because the company raised a lot and stayed frugal, meaning a few million in the bank could be returned to the investors. Also, Jack and his co-founder had control of the board, enabling them to negotiate this outcome with the investors successfully.

Nic Brisbourne sees startups occasionally return capital to the investors, which he considers the right thing to do in some circumstances:

> "If the issue is that product market fit can't be found,

> or there's any underlying issue in business which can't be fixed with execution, then it doesn't matter who's in charge; the company most likely isn't going to succeed. Then you're definitely better off returning capital."

Suppose you do find yourself in a situation where you don't see yourself running the business anymore, the company hasn't found product-market fit, and there is a meaningful amount of money in the bank. In such a situation, returning money to investors could be a potential way forward.

IF YOU DECIDE TO STAY

As I've said before and will keep repeating, don't sit on the fence. If you decide to step down, that's perfectly fine, and if you choose to stay, that's a valid decision. So, what if you decide to remain as the CEO of your company?

First of all, congratulations. Nearly all founders, at some point, will consider stepping down. It's understandable. Running startups is hard. It's okay to have doubts and wonder if it's the right thing for you right now. And so it's a big deal that you thought about it carefully and decided to keep running your business.

The significance of this moment is that it holds the promise of clarity, of not waking up the next day wondering if you should write a resignation letter, of not being distracted by this process. Congratulations, you are not sitting on the fence anymore.

How confident are you, though? Have you really decided, or will you change your mind next week or next month, returning to square one, sitting on the fence again? You can do a few things to check if you have really decided to stay.

Write down your story. No one has to see it, although you might choose to share it with your trusted circle of supporters. Write about how you started your business and what inspired you to take the risk.

Write about the reasons you were seriously considering stepping down. Explain the concerns, and describe how you addressed them and chose to stay as the CEO. If you felt like leaving because of the stress, what will ensure that you work more sustainably as the business continues to grow through inevitable challenges?

What are other practical implications of deciding to stay? If you firmly decide to stay as a CEO, what will you do next? Paint a picture of where you and the business will be in a few years' time. What are you going to do this year and next year? Will you be more ambitious in product development or fundraising? Will you make changes at the senior level? What must be different to address the concerns that prompted you to consider stepping down?

Reflect on what you would like to keep an eye on to ensure you don't have to face this decision again soon. If you considered stepping down because of the pressure on your mental health or relationships, what boundaries will you set going forward? What signs will help you to avoid falling into the same trap? What accountability structures will you find helpful?

What might prompt you to reconsider your decision? How will you know that the situation has sufficiently shifted? Reflecting on what needs to change so that you can review the decision can give you confidence that you are on the right track.

Record the story on your smartphone and play it back to yourself. What is it like to listen to it? Notice how you feel. Is there joy or sadness, excitement or dread in your voice? Is it a decision that you're proud of or something you're secretly regretting already? Does this decision make you bigger or smaller? When you tell your kids about your doubts and the outcome, do you imagine them being inspired or disappointed?

Share your thoughts with others. Ask for their feedback and listen non-judgmentally. Of course, some of them will disagree with you, maybe even most, but you aren't seeking agreement. You are looking for blind spots, mistakes in your reasoning and feelings you haven't noticed or honoured yet. This isn't decision-making by committee; it's you making a decision, taking as much input as possible to ensure you don't miss anything.

And finally, sleep on it many times. Give it some time and see how it feels. A promising sign that it was a good decision is a long-lasting feeling of relief, lightness and a renewed focus on building a great business instead of endless hesitation.

The mistake I made when I was still CEO was not following my own advice and not writing such a story when I really should have.

I remember that moment. Feeling exhausted and confident that I should step down and hire someone else to run the business, I took a long-planned vacation in Peru. I wasn't very interested in visiting Machu Picchu, but I was looking forward to a two-week ayahuasca retreat deep in the jungle of Amazonia.

Ayahuasca, if you have never heard about it, is a potent plant medicine that's traditionally been used in South America for spiritual journeys, thanks to its psychoactive effect causing an altered perception of reality. Over two weeks, a group of fellow travellers and I, under the guidance of a local shaman and a Buddhist teacher from the States, took part in seven ceremonies, journeying through the depths of our unconscious to bring clarity to whatever was vexing each of us.

We did yoga in the mornings, took flower baths at lunchtime and enjoyed walks in lush rainforest before gathering after dark to meditate and start a ceremony that would last until the morning hours, taking us to places I never knew existed.

One of the intentions I brought to the retreat was to find clarity on my situation and my next professional steps. I didn't expect Mother Ayahuasca to give me the answers, but I was looking for a new perspective.

The new perspective did arrive, indeed. I have yet to read a description of a psychedelic journey that would give it justice, so I will not attempt it, but I'll say that at the end of my retreat, I called my friend Rob to say that I didn't have any intention to step down anymore. There was no particular reason; I didn't want to do it anymore. Quite the opposite, I was looking forward to returning to the office to continue running the business.

And that's what I did. I flew back to London with clarity of mind. I never felt as good about running the company as I did in the following two months. I was happy, productive, energised, and genuinely looking forward to business meetings and new challenges.

Until I wasn't, of course. About two months later, I was back to square one. I thought I had clarity, but nothing changed since I hadn't actually addressed any of the underlying issues that got me thinking about stepping down in the first place.

And so when the board asked me how the transition plans were going, I kicked into gear. This time, I knew for sure what the right thing to do was.

IF YOU DECIDE TO STEP DOWN

If, after careful deliberation, you decide to leave, congratulations, too. There's no shame in stepping down. There's no glory in doing the job you shouldn't be doing. You have only one life to live, and it's up to you to decide how to live it. What matters is that you are not sitting on the fence anymore.

Sometimes, what crystallises the decision is finding the right person. As Flavia, a founder in transition who's currently preparing to hand over to her successor, said:

> "The doubts ended when I found the right person. Prior to that, I was going through the motions with someone else, and there was another candidate who I had nearly hired. I stopped myself because I saw the pattern repeating itself: 'You're just going with this person because you want to get out. But you're torn and conflicted because you know he's not the right person for the business.' Whereas now I know he is right."

Even if you're confident, all the advice in the previous section still stands. Make sure you are as confident as you can be and clear about the reasons. Write it down. Read it back to yourself. Discuss it with others. Unlike the decision to stay as CEO, this one is generally irreversible.

Every so often, we face a decision that will have long-lasting consequences. To move to a different country. To marry. To divorce. To have kids. To start a business. Stepping down as a CEO is one of such big decisions. Okay, maybe not as big as having kids, but the stakes are still high.

Once you are sure your decision to step down is right, take a deep breath. In a way, a big part of the transition is behind you. You reflected profoundly and made a decision. But in another way, it's only just beginning.

As we discussed in this chapter, there are actual costs to indecision. It's important not to sit on the fence indefinitely, unsure if you want to stay or go. While this decision should not be rushed, procrastinating on it would be a mistake, too. Our job as CEOs is to identify significant impediments to our performance. Our indecision is likely to be one of those.

However, stepping down is not a binary choice. Other options may be appropriate in some circumstances, including returning money to investors. This is why it's essential to understand not only whether you want to step down but also what it means for you.

Finally, once you make a decision, congratulations. It really is a significant milestone on this journey. If you choose to step down, you can now turn your attention to the mechanics, starting with how to take charge of the process and communicate it to others, as we'll discuss in the next chapter.

Questions to reflect on:

- How can you avoid both haste and delay in making this decision?
- What are the personal and professional implications of the decision to step down or stay for you?
- How might your departure impact the company's culture, operations, and future direction?
- What criteria or signals can you use to gauge the correctness of your decision?
- Who in your circle or network can provide reassurance and support?

CHAPTER 5

KICK OFF THE PROCESS

It is important to reflect deeply on why you may want to step down and then decide if you want to do it, but eventually, you must take action. Reflection must precede action, and action must follow reflection.

In this chapter, we'll discuss how to kick off the process by bringing other people into it, particularly the board of directors. We will talk about the importance of taking charge of the process and maintaining trust at the top level — two factors influencing how well the transition will go.

We will also discuss the timing. There is never a perfect time to step down as CEO, but some moments are better than others, especially if your business regularly raises investment funds to finance growth.

An excellent outcome to aim for at this moment in your journey is you being in charge of the process and the board being aligned around what is happening and why. This will put you in a good position to choose or at least significantly influence the choice of your successor.

RECOGNISE WHEN IT'S TIME

Nearly every founder CEO who stepped down remembers

when they decided to do it. I remember sitting across the table from Claudia Harris OBE, then my chair, at Granger & Co. in Clerkenwell, a fancy London café where we met for business breakfasts, and telling her I would need to step down one day.

The night before, we closed a funding round, and the cash hit the bank as we ordered our coffees. Instead of feeling relief, I felt like I ran out of options. My marriage had collapsed, I was utterly exhausted, and I was seeing a psychiatrist that afternoon to talk about my mental state.

I still had enough energy to lead the business until a new CEO would be in place, so it wasn't a resignation. Instead, it was simply a realisation that neither was I the best person for the job anymore, nor was the job right for me.

For other CEOs, the moment of realisation feels less dramatic. A successful, bootstrapped, international company founder found himself looking out the window during a meeting with his finance team, wondering if this is what he should be doing with his life. Living a jetsetter lifestyle, he spent less time with his kids than he would have liked. 'How much money is enough?' he wondered.

Every founder who chooses to step down arrives at that realisation in their own way. However, once you've decided to step down, you'll need to take the first step to make it happen. Let's dig into how to do it.

TAKE CHARGE OF THE PROCESS

One good reason not to sit on the fence for too long, unsure whether to step down, is that we never know how much time we have to make up our minds. Many founders lose control of their boards after raising institutional capital, meaning the board can fire them.

From a somewhat cynical point of view, venture capitalists insist on being on the board to fire you if needed. They don't need to be board members to monitor their investment, and they certainly don't need to be board members to help with introductions or advice. However, they do need to be board members if they ever decide to fire you, and that's why venture investors usually strongly insist on having a board seat.

Deciding whether to back the CEO or replace them is one of the most critical responsibilities of a board of directors. Jonathan Lerner, partner at Smedvig Ventures, explains how investors think about replacing a founder CEO for underperformance if the board has concerns about the CEO's ability to turn things around:

> "As soon as you're not performing against budget, that clearly puts you in more of a danger zone than if you're performing against budget. But I think most investors know there are a million different reasons for this. It's all about how much confidence people have that this team are taking all the right actions to make the company to perform."

However, the board might fire the founder CEO for reasons unrelated to performance. A private equity investor at the Series B stage or later may decide that a 'tried and tested' professional CEO they know will do a better job without waiting for the founder CEO to show any weakness.

Navigating the relationship with a hostile board could be a subject for a different book, but one aspect is relevant here. If you are going to step down anyway, it can be preferable to do so voluntarily instead of being asked to do so.

Jeff Lynn chose to take control of the process himself when he decided to hire his replacement:

> "A lot of difference between voluntarily and involuntarily stepping down is just timing. If I were right in my thinking that someone else would make a better CEO for the business, then, eventually, the board would have figured it out, too. And instead of me going to the board saying, 'This is what I'd like to do', it would have been the board coming to me saying, 'This is what you have to do'. Then, that becomes a much more complicated situation."

While in some cases, the news truly comes out of the blue for the founder, in situations where the founder is struggling, both they and the board usually know it long before either party makes the big decision. If the founder CEO isn't fully committed to continuing in their job, they never know how much time they have.

A founder CEO leaving voluntarily can choose the transition timing that works both for them and the business. They are much more likely to be involved in picking the successor and it will be easier for them to negotiate their future role, for example, as a board member.

It's safe to say that no board looks forward to firing a CEO. By taking the initiative when there is still room for manoeuvre, the founder CEO can make it easier to find a win-win solution for everyone: the business, the board and themselves.

It's essential to take legal advice to understand the implications of stepping down versus being asked to leave, particularly regarding vesting and compensation. The CEO employment contract and investment documents will cover different scenarios and their consequences, as we will discuss later in the book.

There's always scope for negotiating the terms of the departure, and in some cases, taking the initiative may strengthen the founder CEO's negotiating position.

However, taking the initiative is not always the best option. In some situations, it may be preferable for the board to initiate the CEO transition. Depending on your specific circumstances and legal advice, you will need to decide what's best for you and your business.

SHARE YOUR DECISION WITH THE BOARD

When you decide to step down, you must think about how to share the news with the board if you're taking charge of the process.

As we discussed, it's usually preferable for the founder CEO to start the conversation themselves without waiting for the board to conclude that the CEO needs to be replaced. This gives the founder the initiative and gives them a much greater degree of control over the process.

There are three ways in which founders tend to approach the process. The first option is to start the conversation with the board early on when the founder is thinking about stepping down, but there's no clarity about when they might do it or who might replace them. The message is, "I think I might need to step down one day."

The second option is to bring it to the board when the founder is still committed to running the business for as long as it takes.

The message is, "I think we should discuss my stepping down, but there is no rush."

The third option is to tell the board once there's a plan in place: who'll replace the CEO and when the transition will happen. The message is, "I decided to step down, and this is how it will work."

The first approach aims to build trust with the board by showing the willingness to be open and vulnerable and inviting them to collaborate on the problem. The third approach attempts to give the board certainty about what will happen and keep the initiative. The second strategy tries to balance between the other two.

Rory Stirling explains how he'd like founders to communicate their decisions:

> "I never want to find out about it in a board meeting. I'd always want this to be communicated to me one-on-one, not in a situation where I have to make a formal decision.
>
> The second bad way to communicate this decision would be as an FYI, on the phone, when also communicating ten other things."

Nic Brisbourne prefers founders to open this conversation early to avoid making rushed decisions, too:

> "It's helpful to have notice on these things. Definitely, going in with some options and some kind of plan is good, but I'd really prefer to hear that early in its gestation: Here are some things we might do, which do you think might work best?"

However, Adam Fudakowski, founder of Switchee, who always

saw himself as a serial entrepreneur aiming to start multiple businesses, spending a few years on each one, regretted this approach:

> "I had coffee chats with board members to share my view of myself as a serial founder planning to eventually leave the business. I thought this would comfort them, showing I was thinking maturely about my role. However, it unsettled them and wasn't helpful for the relationship."

A couple of years later, feeling closer to the point when he felt it would be the right time to leave, Adam restarted the conversation with the board, this time offering more detail:

> "When I presented Tom as a potential Head of Strategy who could possibly become CEO, the board was more comfortable. I had lost my co-founder and knew I needed help. Tom was a safe pair of hands, and suggesting him helped manage the transition smoothly. Had I directly told the board I wanted to leave and start a search, it would have been a trickier process."

A few months later, Tom was promoted to the top role once it was clear that he would likely be an excellent CEO.

At Seedrs, Jeff Lynn brought it to the board very early on and found their full support:

> "We raised Series A, and it was time to begin scaling. There was never a moment when I wanted to step away from the business altogether. But it seemed that if I could find the right CEO, I could carve out a role for myself that allowed me to focus on things I was good at.
>
> I went to the board and said, 'I think it's time for a 'grown-up CEO'. I don't want to go anywhere; I'd like to

> become an executive chairman to focus on big bets and corporate governance.'
>
> I'm thoroughly glad I did that for two reasons. One, it was the right thing for the business. The other is that I carved out a perfect role for myself by taking control.
>
> I could have held the position for a couple more years, but then the board would have said, 'It's time to go, Jeff'. And at that point, I would be gone.
>
> I was nervous about how the investors might react, particularly those who invested recently, but they were positive about it. They were reassured by the idea that I remained fully committed to the business. They responded, 'Okay, let's not rush this process. This isn't just about getting a warm body. We need to do it right.'"

I followed the same strategy with my own board, telling them that I would need to step down at some point, but I was still committed to running the business for another couple of years if necessary.

Trust is critical here. If there's trust on both sides of the conversation, and there is time to carefully reflect on different aspects of the situation, it's much easier to find a way forward.

Sometimes, founders choose to leave it until relatively late, possibly because they aren't sure how the board might react. They don't want to come across as unprepared, so they come to the board when they have already decided to step down, have lined up something else for themselves to do after the transition and have chosen their successor, at least in their imagination.

Misguided by the desire to project stability and certainty, they come to the board with a set idea of how the transition should happen. This might surprise the board because they would likely have preferred to be involved in the process earlier. This may lead the board to lose trust in the founder CEO and take control of planning the succession themselves.

Angela, a founder CEO who decided to step down for health reasons, described the moment she shared the news with the board:

> "I told them that I needed to resign. I partially also blamed my health condition. I felt it was easier to explain that I was physically unwell and that I couldn't take the stress anymore.
>
> That backfired a little bit. They totally didn't see that coming. The knee-jerk reaction was, 'Okay, if she's not in it anymore, she needs to go.'
>
> I was shocked and upset because I was fully committed to staying on."

This is a classic prisoner's dilemma dynamic. Imagine two prisoners held in individual cells, unable to communicate. Each needs to decide whether to stay silent or betray the other.

They both know that if they stay silent, they'll get off lightly — say, one year each without an admission of guilt. Each of them also knows that if he betrays the other prisoner but the other stays silent, he will walk free, and his partner in crime will get ten years. However, if both of them betray each other, they will get five years each.

The rational strategy for each prisoner is to betray because it removes the chance of getting ten years. Sadly, following the rational strategy prevents them from getting off lightly, which they would have achieved if both stayed silent.

Something similar happens when a startup CEO decides to step down. They may withhold information for too long if they don't trust the board. If the board members don't trust the CEO, they may be tempted to take matters into their own hands. While both responses may be rational when seen from an individual perspective, they tend to lead to a poor outcome for both parties.

The critical lesson in the prisoner's dilemma is that communication and trust matter. If both prisoners could communicate and trust each other, they would get off lightly. Since they can't, they will both make prison their home for years to come.

In Angela's case, after a few days, when the emotions calmed down, she explained to the board that she was still committed and capable, and they started working together on transition plans.

Sometimes, founders delay this pivotal conversation out of fear of how others might react, which can be unfounded. Brandon, a founder CPO at a high-profile fintech, knew for a long time that he was in the wrong job but felt unable to open up to his co-founders about it for fear of how they might react.

Eventually, they sat down with him and had a very frank conversation, suggesting that he leave his job but stay as a board member. Instead of being confrontational or difficult, it was a moment of relief for everyone.

It allowed Brandon to finally switch careers to do what he truly cares about — climate change, not fintech — and it allowed his startup to hire another CPO. A potentially scary conversation led to an immediate sense of relief and a win-win solution, thanks to the trust that Brandon and his co-founders built over the years.

I recommend taking the risk of being open with the board earlier in the process, getting them involved in it and taking the risk of being vulnerable. If we open this conversation when we are still happy to run this business for at least another year or two, when the reasons prompting us to consider stepping down haven't turned into a crisis yet, we can take the risk. The reward is the chance to navigate this transition together as partners instead of everyone fighting for themselves.

It's best practice to communicate this in a series of face-to-face conversations with each board member, asking them not to share the news until you have spoken to everyone. You may also choose to speak to your chair or lead investor first and then decide together how best to communicate it to everyone on the board. Once everyone has had a chance to process the news, ask follow-up questions and reflect on the implications, the board will be ready to discuss it together at the next board meeting or board dinner.

The key to handling these conversations well is clarity on why you are considering stepping down and how you see it working. What's less likely to go well is trying to involve the board in a protracted soul-searching process to decide if you want to stay as a CEO. This work is crucial but is best done with impartial advisors, coaches, close friends or in solitude before it's brought up at the board level.

In other words, the CEO is responsible for finding clarity about what's happening inside their own mind and heart and what they are trying to accomplish. The board is responsible for clarifying what's happening inside the organisation and how to best navigate the succession. It would be a mistake to try to answer deep personal questions with the board's help or solve organisational challenges without the board's involvement.

MAINTAIN TRUST AT THE BOARD LEVEL

Sometimes, despite everyone's best efforts, CEO transitions don't go as well as everyone hopes for. The most significant factor determining whether a CEO transition goes well, by far, is trust at the board level.

It's much easier to execute a complex negotiation and power transition and keep the company running smoothly when everyone works together towards success, without unproductive conflicts in the boardroom.

Unfortunately, it's not always the case. When one startup was unable to meet its ambitious growth goals after a raise, existing investors insisted that the founder leave and be replaced as a CEO. The choice was stark: either they would invest more capital once the CEO is replaced, or the company would run out of cash.

Alex, the founder CEO, strongly felt that the proposed CEO didn't understand her business. Also, he had never raised venture money despite having run several businesses before. Under heavy pressure from aggressive investors, she decided to give up control, even though, with hindsight, she would have chosen to cut costs to extend the runway.

Her fears proved to be true. The new CEO, not being committed enough and not profoundly understanding the business, quit after just six months, after which the investors, being in control of the business, hired a new face again. It still didn't prevent the company from failing some time later. Reflecting on it, Alex described it as "watching a slow-motion car crash", which was emotionally excruciating for her and her co-founder.

The story's lesson isn't that the company would have been fine if Alex stayed CEO. Ultimately, we don't know that. But it's fair to say that having a complete breakdown of trust at the top level did not help the business to navigate a critical moment. Ultimately, everyone lost: Alex, her co-founder, the investors, two new CEOs, clients and the entire team.

What to do about it? As they say, the time to fix the roof is when the sun shines. You don't build trust, reputation or credibility when you need them. You build them in the years before that. In Alex's case, her mistake was to raise from wrong investors who didn't understand the business and panicked at the first sign of trouble instead of putting faith in the founders they backed. Also, in hindsight, Alex believes she raised too early before the company was ready to scale.

These mistakes are common and not unique to founder transitions, but they point to a simple truth. Challenges are easier to navigate if all stakeholders trust each other. If trust is in short supply during a CEO transition, it's far more likely to go wrong.

CHOOSE TRANSITION TIMING

Another practical consideration is timing. In the ideal world, we would choose the perfect time to transition to the new CEO. However, this is rarely the case because several factors influence this process.

The first one is the decision-making of the CEO (or the board, if it's the board that decides to replace the CEO). As we discussed at the beginning of the book, it's wise not to sit on the fence for too long. Once you notice you're seriously considering stepping down, this will likely impact your well-being and your performance as a CEO. Instead of focusing on the business's success, you might start giving much of your attention to whether you should step down or not. This can be highly distracting because our minds tend to struggle with uncertainty.

Another important factor is the fundraising cycle. If you are building a venture-backed business, you are likely raising a new round every 18-24 months. Raising money if you have announced that you are stepping down is difficult because the investors will, understandably, want fundraising to be led by the new CEO.

However, stepping down soon after you raise a round is not straightforward either. If you hadn't told your new investors before the round that you had planned to leave soon, that would be a breach of integrity that would ruin the trust you have built with your investors. Rory Stirling agrees:

> "The CEO needs to commit to going through that funding round, raising the capital, and then also staying with the company for a period of time after that so that you don't end up in that awful break of integrity situation breaking the news at the next board meeting after the raise."

It's easiest to step down between two fundraising events because that allows you to make progress on your promises to your investors at the last round and gives time and runway to your successor to prepare for the next round.

As a rule of thumb, the company will need at least six months of runway from the moment the new CEO takes over if their immediate task is to start preparing for fundraising, and that assumes they already have a network and experience of going through a venture round. From this perspective, the most convenient time for CEOs of venture-backed companies to step down is every 18-24 months.

One way to align the timing is to have your successor in a holding pattern in a senior role. Adam Fudakowski, whom we met earlier, hired his successor Tom as Head of Strategy for two reasons: to find out what it would be like to work together and to control the timing.

This allowed Adam to speak with the board nearly a year before he stepped down, engaging them in the process. It also allowed him to involve Tom in the next fundraise. This ensured that when Adam told the board that he was ready to step down to be replaced by Tom, the new investors had already had a chance to get to know him.

This way, Adam managed to be open with his board about his plans, avoid surprising new investors, build a working relationship with Tom, and retain control over whether and when he'd step down. As a result, the CEO transition from Adam to Tom happened smoothly in the middle of the fundraising cycle, giving Tom time to prepare for the next round.

The truth is, things are not always this simple. One complication is that it's tough to predict how long it will take to find a successor unless you already have someone suitable.

If you are starting an external search, it's prudent to allow about six months to align the board on the job spec and compensation, choose and instruct an executive search firm, interview several potential candidates, negotiate an offer to one of them and sign the contract. This takes time, and even then, it's not the end.

There's every chance a successful candidate is already employed in a high-profile job with a notice period of at least three months, but more likely six or more months. In my case, it took 14 months, almost to the day, between deciding to step down and signing off Slack.

These two timelines — fundraising and external search — don't align well. If you start the process midway through your fundraising cycle, you might run out of money before you find a great successor. If you start the process before the raise, it might hurt the chances of your raise happening. If you start the process soon after the raise, it will raise the question of whether you misled the investors.

So, there's no easy answer to this question, but there are some considerations that might help.

As discussed above, the most significant factor determining a CEO transition's success is the level of trust at the top. If the founders, the CEO, the board and the investors all trust each other, this alone will help navigate the inevitable challenges that will come up during the transition, including the timing.

The founder CEO's emotional state is another factor that sometimes influences the transition's timing. The trap that founders considering stepping down sometimes fall into is waiting until they don't have any emotional or mental capacity to continue running the business well for another year.

Burnout is real. Many, if not most, startup founders are familiar with its symptoms. The prolonged stress of running an early-stage business for years can and does take entrepreneurs to the point of exhaustion where they want a way out, whatever the costs.

I remember a coaching session with a founder who mentioned in passing that he'd be happy to give up all his vested shares as part of the transition if the investors insisted on not having any "dead equity" on the cap table. I challenged him on this intention, as it sounded excessive. After all, he spent years building this company. Yet, I understood it came from a place of being very tired and even, unjustifiably, guilty.

Choosing to step down as a CEO is not a crime for which founders should pay an arm and a leg; it's simply a change of leadership. However, when we are burned out and tired after years of relentless pressure, we might be tempted to get out at all costs. This leaves little room for flexibility in choosing a successor or negotiating good leaving terms.

A good point to decide to leave the business is when the founder CEO doesn't have to, knowing they can effectively run the business for another year or more.

In reality, it's rarely this simple. It may take considerable time for us to know if our transition timing was optimal.

How and when you choose to kick off the process of CEO transition will influence how it will go. It is usually preferable to take charge of the process instead of letting the board do it because you have the most skin in the game and because it may give you more influence over who takes over after you if you don't control the board.

The most crucial factor to keep in mind is trust at the board level. CEO succession is a delicate process, which can easily fall apart if key decision-makers don't trust each other. Communicating the situation early, openly and honestly will help you build trust with the board.

Finally, the earlier you kick off the process, the more room you will have to choose the right timing. There's no perfect moment to step down, but choosing it wisely will give you more room for manoeuvre, especially when it comes to choosing the successor, as we'll discuss in the next chapter.

Questions to reflect on:

- What's your sense of the level of trust among key stakeholders?
- How can you convey your decision to step down to the board in a constructive way?
- What fears or uncertainties might prevent you from initiating the transition process?
- How does fundraising impact your CEO transition timing?
- What does it mean for you to take charge of this process?

CHAPTER 6

CHOOSE YOUR SUCCESSOR

Few choices you'll make on this journey will be more consequential than choosing your successor. Once you have decided to step down and have started the conversation with key stakeholders, this will be the question on everyone's mind: who will lead the business next?

Over the next few years, the new CEO will have a chance to take your business to the next level or ruin it completely. However, it's not only their skill set that matters. How aligned they are with the rest of the shareholders also matters greatly.

In this chapter, we'll reflect on a few key questions. What should the skill set of the incoming CEO be? Should internal candidates be favoured? Who should run the search process? How to negotiate the compensation? How to get the board aligned around the successor?

What you're looking for is a candidate that all stakeholders are excited by and who has the skills to take the business to the next level in a few years. Once you have identified them, you'll be ready to start planning a smooth transition to the new CEO, which we'll discuss next.

CHOOSE SOMEONE YOU TRUST

As a CEO who chooses to step down, one of the most important decisions you will make or influence is who will replace you. Given that a meaningful part of your net worth is still likely to be locked in the business, even negotiating specific financial terms of your departure isn't as important as the value the new CEO will create (or ruin).

It's not simply about the financial value, of course. Like it or not, our companies will be part of our identity for a while after we step down, and people will recognise us as founders of our businesses long after we step down. As Jeff Lynn said:

> "If you founded a successful business, it doesn't matter if you're the office cat. You will get credit for the fact that it is your business."

If you aren't comfortable with what your successor is doing with the business, if their actions violate your values, that might be a heavy burden to carry. The first example that comes to mind is British entrepreneur Jo Malone, who sold her business to Estée Lauder, giving them the right to continue using her name as a brand, only to bitterly regret some of the actions Estée Lauder took years later, which unfairly reflected on her personally.

Flavia, a founder in transition, considered the impact her successor's actions would have on her reputation, not just the value of her equity:

> "Even if I never make another cent from it, I leave it with a good story. If it crashes and burns, it's my reputation that goes down with it. Then I won't be able to leverage my experience because it'll suddenly be tarnished."

If you remain involved in the business, whether at the board level, as a shareholder, or especially as an employee, you'll spend years working alongside your successor. It's worth considering very carefully who will lead the business after you.

When I started interviewing founder CEOs who stepped down, I was surprised to learn that in most cases, they and their boards preferred to hire someone they already knew instead of doing a full executive search as the default option.

Sometimes, the executive search was performed for good measure after identifying a potential candidate. Sometimes, that candidate was found thanks to the executive search. However, in many, if not most cases, the founders and their boards chose someone they knew and trusted over someone they didn't know, even if they came with brilliant references and an impressive CV.

Intuitively, this makes sense. Trusting the company you built to someone else is exactly that — an act of trust — and we tend to trust people more if we've known them for a long time. Conversely, this means that if you plan to become the CEO of someone else's startup, building long-term trusted relationships with outgoing founders may be a better strategy than courting executive headhunters.

Tom Nixon offers an interesting and useful perspective on the choice of the successor in his book *Work With Source,* building on the ideas of Peter John Koenig and Stefan Merckelbach. Tom argues that behind any successful company is one person, a source, who profoundly and intuitively understands the business's vision and values. Even if the company has several co-founders, only one of them is the source.

It's not a formal role that anyone can be appointed to. However, for the new CEO to know instinctively what needs to be done, they must become the source. This requires a conscious choice and unconditional support of the person who was the original source.

If this transition doesn't happen, the founder, who still feels like they are the source, may find great trouble letting go and focusing on something new. Likewise, the new CEO, not feeling like they are the source, may struggle to hold the vision and command respect and authority. Since this describes more of an energetic dynamic than a formal transfer of a role, this process must be done in parallel with a formal transfer of power.

Regardless of who is chosen to be your successor, it's essential to trust this person. No matter the challenge, it's easier to navigate if there's deep trust at the top level.

HIRE FOR REAL COMMITMENT

Looking back, I see that established trust was the reason why the board of directors at Makers, my own business, also appointed a trusted insider instead of hiring an external candidate.

Having discussed at length my reasons for considering stepping down and the expectations for the successor with the board members, having written the job description, I realised that I should not be the one driving the process as the outgoing CEO. The chair of the board would usually do this job, and thankfully, I had an excellent chair, Claudia, with whom I first discussed stepping down many months before.

Given my respect for her, I might have secretly hoped that Claudia would take over my role, but what were the chances? After all, she was busy as CEO of another business. Yet I also knew that Claudia had a great deputy CEO running the business well while she was on maternity leave. Plus, her business was in good shape, making it easier for the CEO to leave.

In a pivotal conversation at the same café where Claudia and I first discussed my stepping down, I argued that if ever there was a good moment to consider other CEO opportunities, this was it. Would Claudia be open to potentially leading Makers? To my relief, she said she was open to the opportunity.

This put the job of running the process back into my hands, and, together with other board members, we interviewed Claudia, just as we would have done with any other candidate. We spoke about the job, negotiated the compensation, created a transition plan for both companies and ultimately made an offer that was accepted.

There's one moment from this transition that stands out for me. When we started the conversation in early 2020, we didn't know that the virus that would become known as COVID-19 would shut down the economy within weeks. We felt that the company's prospects were bright, and even when the new virus made its way to Italy, overwhelming its hospitals, we didn't fully realise the impact it would have on the rest of the world. Mere weeks later, the country went into a nationwide lockdown.

For our business, that was bad news for two reasons. At the time, we operated two student campuses in London, so moving to a fully remote format on short notice was challenging our operating model. Much more importantly, we are in the business of training and placing junior software engineers, and in the uncertainty of 2020, nearly every business had stopped hiring juniors.

Everyone was, understandably, waiting to see the impact of COVID-19 on the economy. To make matters worse, we had a brand promise to refund students if they couldn't get jobs. When the entire country stopped hiring, the financial liability ballooned overnight, presenting huge risks: financial (if we paid out) and reputational (if we defaulted). But how could we default if our clients, stuck in a lockdown themselves, often really needed that money to pay their own bills, being unable to get work through no fault of their own?

We updated our operating model to shift online in a matter of days and duly executed the necessary cuts. However, we wondered if we'd still have the business in a few months. At that point, only the board knew about the intended CEO succession, and nothing had been signed.

I called Claudia from my spare bedroom, which became a home office during the pandemic, and said, "Claudia, the situation has materially changed. If we have to shut down the company, that's my job to do. It's not what you signed up for. If you'd like us not to go ahead with the CEO transition, I'll stay as the CEO."

I remember Claudia thinking for a few moments and then replied: "Evgeny, I did think that I would be starting on a high note indeed. However, I wouldn't be a good CEO if I were only prepared to be CEO during good times. If I need to start in my role during bad times, that's where the work starts. I'm still in."

At that moment, I knew we had hired the right successor. Needless to say, Claudia successfully navigated successive lockdowns and resulting market changes. Years later, she is still running the business better than I ever could.

HELP YOUR SUCCESSOR INHABIT YOUR PSYCHE

Years later, discussing the transition with Claudia, I came to appreciate how much the job—from her perspective—was defined not by our goals, business model, balance sheet, or even the mission but by how I, her predecessor, saw the world.

A company inevitably expresses the founders' values and worldview, none more so than the CEO. This invisible fabric ties every aspect of the business together, from choosing who to hire to what goals to set, how to manage the team, which customers to target and even the choice of snacks in the office.

Everything that anyone in a startup is doing and how they are doing it is, on some level, a reflection of the psyche of the CEO. It's true for any company of any size, but it's much more pronounced in early-stage startups.

The new CEO, therefore, has to inhabit the psyche of the previous CEO to understand deeply why the company is the way it is and how to run it. The more aligned the two leaders are in their worldviews and values, the easier it will be for the new CEO to authentically maintain the elements of the business they want to keep and change the rest. In Claudia's words, our alignment in how we think about the business allowed her to build on strengths instead of rebuilding the foundation.

Even though we had known each other for years before the CEO transition, thanks to Claudia being our chair, she felt that only about 85% of the "ecosystem," as she described the inner and uncodified aspects of the business, revealed itself to her when she became CEO. The rest was discovered later. The process of taking the seat as the incoming CEO takes months of being immersed in the details.

The goal is not to find a CEO who is as similar to you as possible. The point of hiring a new CEO is to find someone who will chart a new path. A promising startup in the UK was taken to an incredible exit after a new CEO, Sully, an insider, was appointed to run the business. And he did things very differently.

Sully, who was much more commercially minded than the founder CEO, rolled up his sleeves to change many, if not most, aspects of how the business was run and quickly took it to the next level, delivering a significant financial outcome to the founder, the investors and himself.

What enabled him to know what to change and how to do it was a deep understanding of how the previous CEO saw the world. As a member of the senior management team before stepping up, he understood what needed to be kept, what needed to be removed and what needed to be added.

There's a line between being different and being incompatible. Flavia hired an incredible operator to promote him to the CEO role if he performed well. He pored over every detail and significantly improved the company's operating model.

In many ways, Flavia acknowledges that the business is operating well today thanks to his ruthless focus on operational excellence. Yet, it's precisely that ruthless focus that became a problem for the culture and morale, which ultimately led to him leaving the business:

> "He's one of the best operators I've ever met, unbelievably good. But he was the cultural opposite of my startup... And when he eventually left, I had to do a huge piece of work, to move the business from being, culturally, in a very bad place, but operating really well, to operating really well with a good culture again."

We choose our successors, hoping they will do things differently and better than us. It would be wise to accept that we won't always agree with them on every single decision, and that alone doesn't make them a wrong successor.

The way the business looks when it is assessed only through objective measures like financial documents or customer feedback is inherently incomplete. To really understand why things are as they are in this business and how to take it forward, the new CEO will need to learn to inhabit the psyche of the founder CEO.

You can help the new CEO really understand your psyche through many long conversations about why things are as they are. If the new CEO is really interested in how you see the world and the company, I would take it as a good sign.

ALIGN FOUNDERS AND INVESTORS

Who chooses the new CEO? On the face of it, it's up to the board of directors to make the appointment. However, if they leave on good terms and at their own initiative, the outgoing CEO will significantly influence the decision. After all, they have a lot of skin in the game, and they know the job and the culture of the business very well. They are uniquely positioned to have an informed opinion about who will likely be a good CEO.

Suppose the startup is lucky to have experienced investors on the board who have seen several CEO transitions and had a role to play in the recruitment process. In that case, they will also have valuable experience to bring to the table. And even if they haven't navigated a CEO transition before, they will have a perspective to offer.

My invitation to the outgoing founder and investors is to genuinely listen to each other's perspectives during this process. The outgoing founder knows the job but likely has no experience hiring a CEO. The investors on the board might have participated in hiring CEOs before and learned painful lessons, but they don't have as much skin in the game or tacit knowledge of the business as the founder. Both perspectives really need each other.

Then, some co-founders hold a lot of influence in the process, even if they aren't board members. This is because a founder CEO transition inevitably changes the dynamics of the team of co-founders, but also because they are critical to the future success. So, the position co-founders take will also matter a great deal.

Rory Stirling remembers running an exec search process together with two founders of one of his portfolio companies:

> "Founders have value in a company for a lot longer than we think they do, even if they're not in the CEO role. And I believe that these founders needed to be in the company for the company to be successful and valuable. And for that to happen, they needed to run the recruitment process."

It's fair to say that while most regular employees might be less sensitive to who leads the organisation as long as they do it well, co-founders will need to be genuinely on board with the new appointment. If the co-founders are not happy with the appointment of a new CEO, particularly if one of them thought they deserved the position, they might end up leaving the business, voluntarily or not. Alternatively, they may decide to undermine the new CEO's authority by expressing their discontent in indirect ways.

Appointing a new CEO without the full and genuine support

of co-founders who are still operationally involved will likely create later problems.

APPOINT SOMEONE TO RUN THE PROCESS

One board member will be tasked with running the process. If the board has a chair, they are the most obvious candidate (unless they would like to be considered, as happened in my case). It could be the outgoing CEO or one of the other board members with relevant experience.

Regardless of how the process is structured, I recommend agreeing on who's in charge and what the process is. How will the interviews be conducted? Will an executive search firm be involved? How much can the business afford to spend on the search and the package? What are the job specifications and the expectations for the new CEO?

Rory Stirling stresses the importance of using an executive search firm if the business can afford it and doesn't have an obvious candidate:

> "My general view is that Series A and beyond, if you're well capitalised for a senior level search, you want to use an exec search firm, because you end up getting a better pipeline of candidates and it's better run. So it's more likely to get a good outcome."

James Routledge agrees with the importance of investing in executive search, reflecting on his experience of hiring one of his angel investors as a new CEO:

> "A proper recruitment process would have absolutely been the best thing to do. You know, hands down. I don't regret him being the CEO at all. Yet, I do wonder if we'd

> have gotten a recruiter and done a good recruitment process; we'd have learned a lot from that. Because I would have been forced to ask, Who am I actually looking for? What skills do they need to have? What experience do they need to have?"

The person running the process should speak with everyone involved and understand their goals, concerns, and motivations. The more alignment there is at this stage, the less likely the process will fall apart later. For example, it can fall apart over the requirement that the successful candidate ran a startup before or their equity expectations. Lack of alignment can also set up the new CEO for failure after the appointment.

One founder in transition worked hard to create a process to ensure a diverse pipeline of CEO candidates, carefully choosing an executive firm with expertise in this area. At the same time, one of his investors kept making introductions to overrepresented candidates — white men like both of them, — suggesting they be interviewed immediately. Agreeing on how the CEO search process should be run before kicking it off would have prevented much frustration for both of them.

While it is the board's responsibility to appoint the CEO, who else needs to be consulted in the process, even if they can't veto the appointment? Are there any key staff members or advisors who can bring an additional perspective? Considering who needs to know (and who doesn't) beyond the board of directors can bring additional perspectives.

As is the case with any hiring process, the more clarity there is on what a successful CEO appointment looks like and the process that will find them, the easier it will be.

REFLECT ON THE NEW CEO'S MANDATE

Even if there are possible candidates in mind that the board already likes, it would be wise to start by writing a job specification, just like you would for any other position. So, what's the job?

As we discussed at the beginning of the book, the jobs of a founder and a CEO are different. The founder's job is to ensure the startup survives and finds product-market fit. A founder builds the product, talks to customers and hires the early team. A CEO builds the company that builds the product. They hold the vision, build the team and give them resources to execute.

In this book, I assume the transition from the founder to a new CEO happens after the product-market fit. If it happens earlier than that, you are really hiring a new founder and not a new CEO. This is a somewhat different and more complicated process.

Replacing a founder with another founder whose main task is to find the product-market fit before attempting to scale it is difficult for two reasons. The first reason is that finding product-market fit is nearly always very hard. So, the incoming founder might expect to be compensated with the amount of equity that would be not far off from what they'd expect if they started a new business.

From the point of view of existing shareholders who have already invested money, giving up so much equity can feel unfair. It might be tempting to hire someone who'll accept a small equity package and a market salary, but that person may or may not have the skills to take a company to product-market fit. After all, if they can do it, they can go and start their own company.

The second reason is that before product-market fit, most of the value of the business tends to lie in the lessons the founding team learned while discovering what works and what doesn't. This knowledge can't all be written down, so if the founding CEO leaves, they take a big part of it with them.

For this reason, in pre-product-market fit startups, it's almost certainly a good idea to trust the business to one of the remaining founders or early team members. If no one is raring to take the top job, that's probably a sign that the startup is facing not a CEO succession but the death of the business.

Rory Stirling stresses it even more strongly:

> "There is a point at which the company would survive without the founder CEO (i.e. it is technically possible to replace them). I am certain this point is beyond reaching strong product market fit."

So, once product-market fit is found, even though it exists on a continuum and is not a binary event, it becomes far easier to hire a new CEO and write a job specification for them. While every CEO job is different, Fred Wilson's CEO job framework is the best description I've seen:

> "A CEO does only three things.
>
> Sets the overall vision and strategy of the company and communicates it to all stakeholders.
>
> Recruits, hires, and retains the very best talent for the company.
>
> Makes sure there is always enough cash in the bank."

These three points transform into three crucial questions the board must ask. Do we believe in the vision and the strategy the candidate is presenting to us? Do they have a track record of recruiting and retaining top talent? Will they be able to fundraise?

This moment also becomes an opportunity to rethink the job of a CEO because founder CEOs sometimes fail to let go of parts of the job they've been doing since the early days. Maybe they started as a technical co-founder and are still too involved in the technical decision-making, taking some of the responsibilities that their CTO should own.

Or maybe they never learned how to build a scalable sales process and are still involved in the day-to-day of every sales deal, which the incoming CEO probably shouldn't be doing, except if they want to deeply understand the process before delegating it to an executive.

The CEO transition isn't just an opportunity to replace the CEO like-for-like. It's an opportunity to reflect on the CEO's job and what corresponding changes might be needed on the senior management team. Therefore, the starting point should not be the to-do list of the outgoing CEO but clarity on what the new CEO should be doing.

The new CEO's tenure will likely have a different focus from the outgoing CEO, who might have spent years finding product-market fit and only started to scale the business. In this case, the job of the new CEO is to get the business to the next level of scale. Or, maybe the outgoing CEO ran the business for years, and the job of the new CEO is to get the business all the way to the exit. So, what is it that you want the new CEO to accomplish?

It's also a moment to reflect on the experience required. Is it growth experience or working at a large corporation? Will the ideal candidate come from a startup or a public company? Will they need to be great at strategy or leadership? What functional expertise will they need to have? What industries should they know from the inside?

Clarifying what you want the new CEO to accomplish over the next few years will make it much easier to choose the right candidate.

GIVE POTENTIAL SUCCESSORS A TRIAL RUN

One way to decide whether a potential successor is the right person is to hire them in a non-CEO position and later promote them to the top job. This option works well for candidates who prefer to see the business from the inside before committing to leading it.

A CEO appointment that terminates one year in never looks good on a resume unless it's a good exit, so joining in a COO or Head of Strategy capacity could be a way for the candidate and the board to get to know each other.

However, this strategy has its pitfalls. As Flavia discovered during her three attempts to hire a successor, what also matters is the willingness to do the job before the person is promoted into the CEO role if they're initially hired at the C-level.

Her original intention was to hire a C-level executive and spend extensive time working with them before promoting them to the CEO role. However, people who are hired with the intention of being promoted might treat their CxO role as a mere distraction on their way to promotion:

> "This was the biggest mistake that I made. If you go out and interview somebody with the potential that in a year or two or three years' time they become the CEO, what

you end up getting is a lot of candidates that don't want to do the CxO role. They want the CEO role, right?"

Her experience led her to choose a different approach:

> "You need to hire a team around you and then figure out which one of those team members could be your successor without actually telling them that that's what you're doing."

As we'll see in the next chapter, whether you're hiring a new CEO straight away or a CxO with the potential to be promoted one day, building a solid leadership team is one of the critical factors ensuring a successful transition.

DECIDE WHO NEEDS TO KNOW

I generally advocate for more transparency in startups, including at the board level, since few things benefit from a lack of scrutiny. However, discussing the transition and selecting a new CEO is one exception that should be kept under wraps until there's clarity on the outcome.

There are multiple reasons for this. The most obvious is avoiding giving a wrong impression to the team, customers and competitors. It's easy to hear a rumour about the CEO leaving and conclude that the company is not in a strong position or that something must be broken.

In reality, CEO transitions are perfectly normal and happen surprisingly often. Unfortunately, they can raise plenty of unfounded concerns. When you choose to share the news, everyone will immediately think, "What does it mean for me?" The more answers you can offer, the smoother the transition will be.

Fair or not, we need to consider the optics. Flavia is well aware of the stigma surrounding founder transitions and the need to stand her own ground and focus on her own goals and values:

> "I think there's a real stigma sometimes when a founder steps down. People ask, 'What's gone wrong? What's wrong with that person? Why have they left? Were they not good enough?'
>
> The truth of the matter is yes, sometimes we're not good enough, sometimes the board pushes you out. But actually, sometimes you just don't want to do that next stage. It doesn't make you any less ambitious. But if we don't want to take over the world and build a billion-dollar business, we're made to feel as if we are less than, and I am more than. So I needed to work out what that looked like for me, not anyone else."

Another reason to keep things private is to preserve the power of the outgoing CEO while they're still running the business. No one listens to the CEO just because they've got the title. Just like an outgoing president is sometimes called a lame duck because their influence wanes as the end of the term approaches, the outgoing CEO will likely notice a subtle change of dynamics as their team, without any bad intention, tries to figure out who the new leader is and what that means.

They aren't entirely wrong: a new leader will bring new ideas, new ways of working, new goals and processes and, often, new structures, which might result in some of the senior people leaving the business. As a CEO, you want your senior team to focus on the job, not on figuring out who the next person in charge is.

James Routledge agrees:

> "Don't tell your team. It's pointless. Find the space

> to support yourself outside your team: chair, board members, advisors, coaches or communities of startup founders."

In my case, Claudia wasn't available to take over from me for several months after we agreed on it, so I was still running the business, knowing I was on my way out. Since many of a CEO's decisions have long-lasting consequences, Claudia and I agreed to align on the big ones: after all, it would be her living with the consequences of my actions. So, we worked much more closely together as we navigated the transition.

To prepare for the succession, Claudia also started spending more time with the business: for example, joining some of our senior meetings. On the one hand, this wasn't anything out of the ordinary as it fell within the remit of her role as a chair. On the other hand, one of our more astute executives later told Claudia and me that he had realised she was taking over as a CEO months before the official announcement, thanks to this slight change in how we worked.

Jeff Lynn was also aware of how the insiders can notice subtle changes:

> "So we never made an official statement about the plan, but the savvier members of the team picked it up. It wasn't any secret; I wouldn't have lied if someone had asked; I just thought we'd have lost some of the value if we'd announced it publicly first."

Earlier in the book, I recommended not bringing personal existential questions to the board of directors, raising the topic only once there's a degree of internal clarity. Likewise, the best practice is to share the news of the CEO transition with the entire team once there's clarity on what it means for everyone.

EXPLORE UNCONVENTIONAL CANDIDATES

There's a reasonably established search process or a pool of candidates for many roles. For example, if you want to hire a CFO, you consider people with accounting qualifications who have progressed through increasingly senior finance roles in your industry. However, when choosing a new CEO for a startup, there are few hard and fast rules. As long as you end up with a candidate who takes your startup to new heights, it doesn't matter where they came from.

Let me illustrate this with a case study of Opus Recruitment Solutions, a mid-sized business that was bootstrapped by its founder to international scale and respectable profitability, only for him to start wondering if he wants to run it for another decade.

The founder, Darren Ryemill, had a trusted insider who knew the business in and out. They were good colleagues and old friends. He was capable and dedicated and had Darren's trust. He might have been a perfect succession candidate, except for one thing: Darren wanted someone who would take the company in a new direction and make its culture more modern and dynamic, all while maintaining its profitability and increasing the enterprise value. The internal candidate was a safe pair of hands to keep the status quo, but he wasn't the kind of candidate Darren had in mind.

Darren was reluctant to run an executive search process because he wasn't sure how to articulate what he was looking for. Different, but safe. New, but trusted.

One day, at an industry event, Darren met Amy Golding, who, on paper, didn't tick all the boxes. Amy had never been in a senior leadership position. She had a consulting background.

Amy was very intelligent and incredibly hard-working, but was that enough to run a company with hundreds of staff?

Darren ended up hiring Amy on a fixed-term contract to do a piece of strategy work for the business. While genuinely helpful, the real intention of the engagement was for Darren and Amy to get a chance to work together and for Amy to get to know the business and the team. By the end of the consulting engagement, Darren was confident she was the right person for the job. It won't be surprising that the internal candidate left soon after Amy's appointment, unwilling to continue in the second role under a new leader.

A few years later, Amy took Darren's business to a successful exit, delivering an outstanding return to both.

I like this story as a case study because it breaks every single "rule" of hiring a CEO successor. The company had a trusted insider but chose to hire externally. The founder could have engaged an executive search firm but instead trusted his gut. The successful candidate stepped into her role as a leader of a few hundred people worldwide, having run only small teams before.

However, two rules were not broken, which might have been the most important. The first rule is finding a person you can deeply trust your business to. The second rule is to get out of the way, which we'll discuss in the next chapter, where I'll return to this case study to explain how Darren and Amy worked together.

Darren and Amy spent months building trust, working together and learning about each other. After a few months, it didn't matter that Amy didn't fit the profile of a stereotypical CEO candidate and hadn't considered scale-up CEO positions earlier in her career. What mattered was that Darren and Amy trusted each other, worked together well, were aligned on the goals, and had the skills to make it happen.

PREPARE THE RIGHT COMPENSATION PACKAGE

Just like I was surprised to learn that trust played such an essential role in different CEO transitions, I was also surprised to learn how little attention was paid to the question of the overall package for the incoming CEO, both by the boards and by the candidates.

Time and time again, when I asked incoming and outgoing CEOs how they were approaching negotiating the package, they would wave off the question as something insignificant. "I don't quite remember; we discussed it, and then we agreed on something reasonable" was a common reply.

Just like with trust, it makes sense because, for both parties, there is far more than money at stake. A new CEO is committing the next many years of their life to this startup. The outgoing CEO is primarily concerned with whether this is the right candidate or not. Of course, there is a negotiation, and both parties try to find a fair, win-win solution. Still, I haven't encountered a single example where an otherwise promising appointment would fall through because the parties could not agree on compensation. Where there's a will, there's a way.

However, just because two parties agree on the package doesn't mean they won't regret it later. One CEO who replaced the founder CEO took the business to an impressive exit seven years later. Still, when she negotiated the equity package, she assumed it would take only two or three years.

Even though she did well for herself, she later wondered if it was fair that both she and the founder CEO each spent about seven years running the business before the exit, but the founder got most of the money. She might have negotiated her equity harder had she known she was in for a seven-year commitment.

Various industry reports provide a guideline for what's appropriate at the current stage of the business. One of them is prepared regularly by Upscale Partners, an executive search firm in the UK. They provide a salary breakdown for non-founding startup CEOs by stage (seed / Series A / B / C) and equity and bonus data. A similar report is prepared by Erevena, a different executive search firm.

As of this writing, the latest 2023 report by Upscale Partners shows an average basic salary for non-founder startup CEOs in the UK of £175,500 (although it can go as high as £274,000), 5.8% in equity and an average bonus of 40%.

If your startup has professional venture capitalists on the board, they will undoubtedly have access to insider information about appropriate compensation for a given situation. Any executive search firm with extensive experience headhunting startup CEOs will be able to provide a recommendation for your business, taking into account the industry, size, candidate background and other factors.

As a general rule, incentives drive outcomes. Typically, the package will be weighted towards equity to encourage increasing enterprise value and delivering a significant exit for the shareholders. However, if the company is not venture-backed and the new CEO intends to optimise for predictable free cash flows, the compensation structure should reflect this.

It's also important to remember that the new CEO will look at factors other than salary, bonus, and equity, just like any other employee. Factors like health insurance, work flexibility, and parental leave policies must be considered.

A vesting schedule that describes how quickly the promised equity vests (typically 4-6 years with a one-year cliff, allowing the board and the CEO to part ways within the first year if things go wrong, without spending precious equity) will likely be one of the negotiation points.

Additionally, it's worth leaving room for regular renegotiation of the package and its structure as market conditions, the board's risk appetite, and the company's results change.

Another important factor is ensuring the CEO's compensation is aligned with the rest of the organisation. While the new CEO must be compensated fairly, the rest of the team, starting with the senior management, needs to feel that it's fair in light of their compensation. The new CEO will inevitably have many challenges to address on day one, and fighting the team's impression that they are an overpaid fat cat doesn't have to be one of them.

Not every company has full pay transparency, but in my experience, businesses rarely fully succeed in hiding what everyone is paid, so it's prudent to assume that the details will be known, at least to the senior management.

While the package is unlikely to be the make-or-break factor for the right candidate who likely wants the job just as much as you want to hire them, it's worth thinking carefully about what outcomes you want to incentivise with the structure of the package.

CONSIDER YOUR CO-FOUNDERS

If a co-founder is willing to step into the top job, they will inevitably be seriously considered, which is rarely an easy choice.

In many cases, they have one incredible strength and one significant weakness. The evident strength is that they co-founded the company. Co-founders have a special relationship with the business. They understand how it works deeply, are more committed to the mission than hired guns, and have had a chance to earn the trust of the team and the board.

Co-founders are more than just insiders. They have spent years thinking deeply about the problem the business is trying to solve, went through blood, sweat, and tears to achieve results and feel more invested in the business than anyone else purely because it's their baby.

Since they have been influencing the business as a founder even if they weren't the CEO, they will likely ensure cultural continuity and make the transition easier for the organisation as they are a known quantity for the team.

However, they are likely to have a significant weakness. If, based on their background, skills, and ambitions, they are an obvious candidate for the CEO role in this business, it would have happened already when the company was formed, and the co-founding team implicitly or explicitly decided who would be CEO. They would need to persuade the board that they will master the learning curve fast enough, given that they likely have never had a CEO job before.

Here's the problem. Suppose the company is doing pretty well, and the CEO is stepping down for reasons that aren't performance-related. In that case, it strengthens the case for hiring someone with experience leading a functional, scaling organisation. The founder's deep commitment and intimate knowledge of the business start looking less attractive if they have never raised money as a CEO, and Series B or C is on the horizon.

Suppose the company isn't doing well, and the previous CEO is leaving partially or fully for performance reasons. In that case, this raises the question of why the potential new CEO has been around for years and hasn't been able to address these challenges. Will they be able to if they get the top job? Will they be able to offer a new vision or a turnaround plan they haven't thought about before? Blaming problems on the predecessor is rarely a wise approach and is never a complete story, especially if it's coming from a co-founder.

As with all aspects of CEO transitions, there are no hard and fast rules for replacing one co-founder with another as a CEO. Yet, in my experience, it's rarely an easy choice. If it were, it probably would have been made years ago.

As a rule of thumb, the more work is needed to find or refine the product-market fit, the more relevant a founder's skillset will be. If the company is further ahead, the case of promoting a co-founder will probably look weaker.

Like with many aspects of CEO succession, there's no simple algorithm to choose the right successor for you. There are rules of thumb that we touched on in this chapter, and there are situations when you must trust your instinct and go for the person who feels right over someone who looks great on paper.

However, at the end of the search process, you should feel as if you can't wait to hand the keys to the business over to them because you're so excited about the impact they'll make — the sooner, the better!

Now that the search, negotiation and aligning the board around the right candidate are behind you, it's time to ensure the handover goes as smoothly as possible.

Questions to reflect on:

- What specific qualities, skills, and experiences should the next CEO possess?
- How do the insights and familiarity with the company culture an internal candidate offers compare to the fresh perspectives and different skills an external candidate might bring?
- Who is best positioned to oversee the CEO search process?
- How can you ensure all stakeholders are supportive of the succession plan?
- When would it make sense to hire a CxO with the intention of promoting them?

CHAPTER 7

PREPARE A SMOOTH TRANSITION

It will be a great relief to have hired a new CEO, but before you can shut down your laptop, you have one last big job to do: help ensure a smooth transition from yourself to the new CEO.

You will have many practical tasks like negotiating your departure terms and rebalancing the cap table. However, one of the most essential parts of this stage is getting out of the way of your successor. As a CEO, you've spent years doing things. What is needed now is the opposite: letting go of your responsibilities and enabling the new CEO to step into power.

Once you have prepared the business to be taken over by your successor, announced the change to the team and the world and resolved all the practical challenges, you'll finally be ready to take a break. There's an art to taking rest as an ex-CEO, as we'll be discussing in the following chapter.

YOUR JOB IS TO GET OUT OF THE WAY

If you only take one idea from this chapter, let it be this: when the transition begins, the old CEO should get out of the way of the new CEO and support them as they prepare to take over. This doesn't necessarily mean leaving; it means not undermining the new CEO.

I know from personal experience that this is not easy. In 2020, I was preparing to hand over the CEO role to Claudia, who was then my chair. I needed to move quickly because the situation was changing fast (isn't it always the case in startups?), and Claudia, not in the CEO seat yet, could only spend limited time and energy to ensure we were always aligned.

This put me in a tricky situation because I couldn't run every decision past Claudia — there were too many — and yet she would be living with the consequences after she took over as CEO. At the time, I saw two options available to ensure we navigated the transition smoothly.

One option would be to bring Claudia's starting date forward by a few months, maybe in a part-time capacity. This was difficult because of Claudia's other significant commitments and because a CEO starting in a part-time capacity would have limited time and attention but would certainly bear full responsibility for the organisation.

The other option entailed committing to align our thinking as closely as possible, while also maintaining the flexibility to act swiftly when required. In the end, we went with it and, in hindsight, made the right call. I did my best to consider Claudia's preferences when running the business, and I could sense that Claudia trusted me to make decisions without discussing every single one with her.

Working closely together during the few months before Claudia formally took over allowed me to get out of the way the day I stepped down as a CEO. The handover documents were written, legal documents were signed, goodbyes were said, and access to all systems was arranged.

On my last official day as the CEO, I shut down Slack (the ops team duly kicked me out a few days later and asked me to return the laptop), set an autoresponder to my work email, and went surfing on the Algarve's west coast.

That day, the most important thing I could do to serve the company was to get out of the way.

CLARIFYING YOUR NEW RESPONSIBILITIES

While every startup CEO transition is different, the outgoing founder CEO needs to be clear about their new role.

Let's return to the previous chapter's example of Darren and Amy. Since Darren's business was bootstrapped, he didn't have a formal board of directors to override him. The ultimate decision-making power stayed with him as the largest shareholder, whether he was the CEO or not. As both of them told me independently, the most important agreement Darren and Amy made was that the only time Darren would override Amy would be when he would choose to fire her.

This is an approach any board and any ex-CEO would be wise to take. The job of the board (or the business owner, in Darren's case) is to appoint and support the CEO. If they don't have confidence in the CEO, they should replace the CEO. But overriding their decision-making is the worst option.

If the new CEO feels any unwelcome influence from the outgoing CEO, they will feel like they aren't trusted to do their job. The outcome will inevitably be frustrating for everyone because neither the new CEO nor the outgoing CEO will feel they have the freedom to execute. If you're out, you're out. Don't quit as a CEO if you want to keep running your business.

Jeff Lynn reflected after stepping down as a CEO:

> "One of the key things about having the ex-boss and the boss work together is that it's always really important that the new boss runs the company and that is never to be challenged in public. At the same time, it's great that [the new CEO] has always been open to being privately challenged."

Vishal, a founder CEO, decided to hire an MD to run the business day-to-day instead of him so that he could focus only on the bits he liked without having a formal CEO title.

Months later, he found himself as busy as before (just with slightly different things) and frustrated that he didn't have direct control over the business. To make it more frustrating, despite his attempts to delegate his work to the new MD, his board still saw him as the person in charge and held him accountable, not the MD.

"Have you really stepped down?" I asked. Not really, it turned out. Instead of feeling free to focus on his other interests, he was under the same pressure but with less control over running the business.

Likewise, Linda, a CEO hired to replace the founder of a biotech startup who stepped down to join the senior management team, realised soon enough that while she had the title, the founder CEO didn't intend to relinquish control. About a year and a half later, feeling unable to do her role without full decision-making authority, Linda stepped down as a CEO, and the founder stepped back in.

While Linda is proud of the business's progress under her watch and the impact she made, she wishes she had a much more detailed conversation with the founder about where the lines of responsibility and power would lie. Clarifying everyone's expectations might have allowed them to find a different way to collaborate.

With hindsight, it's fair to say that this business genuinely needed Linda's skills. It wasn't the case of the new CEO not working out and getting replaced, as it occasionally happens. However, it might have been a mistake to hire her as CEO if the founder was not ready to meaningfully reduce the scope of his responsibilities despite the change of title.

James Routledge regretted not having a clearly defined role after he stepped down as a CEO to remain in the business full-time as a founder without a specific role on the senior team.

> "I don't know if Chris [the new CEO] and I ever fully agreed on my role. Was he willing to take advice from me? Was I willing to report to him? We worked well together; we got on well. Although, it didn't help that the people on the management team were asking, 'Well, what does James do? Why are you here?'
>
> It was easy for me to end up feeling like a spare part, or that what I was doing wasn't important, or that it was just a bit of play whilst everyone else was working on important stuff."

Discussing my transition out of the CEO seat with Claudia two years after the fact, she described the importance of feeling like I was there to help Makers succeed on her terms, not mine.

The way I saw it, Claudia's terms became my terms. The best

way to make the transition successful and ensure the success of the business was to get out of the way and support Claudia as the new CEO, even if sometimes we disagreed in private.

In practice, for Claudia and me, it meant, as I described in the previous chapter, coordinating our thinking on the biggest topics, remembering that it would be her living with the consequences of the decisions made during the transition period. It also meant getting out of the way after I stepped down and focusing on my new role as a non-executive director.

Like Claudia and I, Jeff Lynn worked alongside the new CEO before he was formally promoted to the top job:

> "During that time, we basically co-ran the business. Week in and week out, [the new CEO] was increasingly taking on more and more responsibilities, and I was shifting more towards the work I wanted to do as chairman. So having that transition period of working together was a critical element in the success."

Another founder who stepped down as a CEO negotiated to stay as a senior team member for six months to oversee a functional area she'd been particularly close to. Soon afterwards, COVID hit. Like so many companies, her business decided to cut costs through redundancies.

The depth of the redundancies is a judgment call for a CEO who aims to balance the pain of losing valuable team members with the benefits of extending the runway. In that case, the new CEO and the old CEO disagreed on how deep to cut, which was understandable given that the old CEO hired many of those at risk.

Looking back, the founder reflected that her trying to influence the new CEO to do what she thought was best added another challenge for the new CEO, slowing things down.

In short, whether you stay involved as a board member, a member of the executive team or simply as a shareholder after you step down as a CEO, your best course of action is to support the new CEO from the day it's agreed they'll be taking over. However, according to Nic Brisbourne, founders who stay behind in a genuinely supportive role are a minority:

> "If they are completely on board with the transition, and it doesn't upset them when someone else is playing with their train set, but all the signals are in different places, then it can be hugely helpful to have them around, definitely. And you see that in a decent minority percentage of cases."

As a founder, if you feel an urgent need to override the new CEO, this means one of two things. Either you should restrain yourself and return to being helpful, or they are failing at their job, and the board should replace them.

However, getting out of the way without providing enough support would be a mistake too. Angela, a founder who hired another CEO to lead the business in her place, later wished she stayed around for a bit longer:

> "We had a very sharp cut-off. It was about a week that we overlapped on the payroll. In hindsight, I've learned, of course, that a lot of people overlap for longer. And maybe the risk with that is an ambiguity within the team. Who's actually calling the shots? But, what happened with us was that I felt like many things got lost."

So, there are two considerations to balance here. On the one hand, getting out of the way and supporting the new CEO is essential. On the other hand, it's important to do a good handover, sharing the knowledge you accumulated and being there to answer questions your successor might not have until they actually start the job.

In my experience, most of this work can and should be done while you're still technically a CEO so that when a new CEO formally takes over, they can firmly stand on their own two feet on day one. The previous CEO visibly hanging around after they stepped down may give an impression that the new CEO cannot lead the company by themselves.

PREPARING THE BUSINESS FOR THE TRANSITION

Apart from the choice of the successor and the founder CEO getting in the way of their successor, another critical factor influencing the transition is the shape of the business. A smooth transition is far easier if the business is in good shape.

The most important factor is that the board of directors is aligned on the goals for the business, the high-level strategy to get there, and, therefore, the expectations for the incoming CEO. All other problems can be navigated more easily if there's clarity and alignment at the top level around what the business is trying to achieve. Is the next big goal reaching profitability? Or is it raising a big round? Or is it optimising for predictable cash flows? Or is the board divided on these questions and trying to avoid conflict, with each member hoping to sway the situation their way, given a chance?

Lack of clarity around goals or alignment at the top level might prevent even the best-qualified candidate from doing a great job if the job they are hired to perform differs from what some board members want to do. In this situation, they will be set up for failure, even if the company is, by and large, in a good position and has all the other ingredients for success.

Another important factor is the strength of the management team. While it's the job of a CEO to build and run their management team, if they have to rebuild it as soon as they start on top of all other challenges on their hands, it might set them back considerably, especially when they don't yet know the business inside-out.

A good candidate will correctly prioritise and address the challenges, but it might come at the cost of significant time lost and cash burned. If you want your successor to fly, give them the tools to execute fast. A competent senior team is one of the main tools.

Then there is also the runway. For example, if the business needs to raise debt or make cuts to extend the runway, it may be easier for the outgoing CEO to do this than for a brand new person to take on fundraising or cuts as their first task. If this is something that the outgoing CEO can take off their plate, the new CEO will have more freedom and flexibility, allowing them to focus on taking the company to the next level.

The last factor is operational transparency and preparedness of the business to be taken over. If the new CEO is aware of all potential issues, all documents are in place, and there is clarity on how the business operates, it will make their task much easier.

In my case, as I was leaving, one of the last tasks I did was to build, together with our Head of Finance, a financial model of our potential liabilities to students who weren't getting jobs during COVID lockdowns and who we promised to refund in case they didn't get a job. It was an area of potential concern that was much easier to address for me as the outgoing CEO than for the new CEO because I could see the complex interplay between different variables in that model.

Suppose the board is aligned on the goals and strategy, the executive team is ready to execute well, there's enough runway to avoid immediate fundraising, and the business is ready to be handed over. In this case, the new CEO has a perfect opportunity to take it to the next level.

Of course, the reality is never perfect. The boards can have profound disagreements, the senior team may be dysfunctional, and the bank balance may be low. Perhaps these are precisely why the CEO transition is happening in the first place, and that's okay. However, setting up the incoming CEO for success is worth trying.

THE IMPORTANCE OF DUE DILIGENCE

Every time a startup raises money, investors perform due diligence to ensure they know the actual state of the business they are investing in. Likewise, it should be performed by the new CEO who's about to take over.

As I was preparing to step down, neither Claudia nor I knew that in the background, someone inside the business was preparing to commit financial fraud.

It came to the surface four months into Claudia's role as CEO. She called me to brief me on the situation, and we jumped into action together. Within hours, we established the scale of the fraud and key events leading to it, notified the police, briefed our board, and explained what was happening to the entire team. We kept everyone informed daily during the first week as we dug deeper into the situation.

Looking back, I'm so proud of how well we navigated it. Claudia and I built a culture of trust and transparency at Makers, which allowed us to be very open with the team about the crisis. Even though, at first, it seemed we'd be unable to regain access to our banking systems in time for the Christmas payroll, our team kept calm and carried on. Our efforts paid off: we recovered the money, secured access to our systems and paid everyone on time.

This moment made me realise that I unwittingly handed over a major problem to Claudia, which I should have uncovered myself when I was still running the business. While the fraud didn't cause significant damage, largely thanks to the security controls in place, it was also true that it happened because the security controls I set up were insufficient.

Claudia trusted me to disclose everything I knew about the business, but I didn't know about the fraud. In hindsight, I wonder if we should have made an effort to conduct a light due diligence process that might have uncovered some irregularities in our finances that went unnoticed by me at the time or lapses in our security protocols.

Other incoming CEOs also asked themselves this question, having uncovered some problems weeks or months after taking over the business.

Sully, a professional CEO hired to lead a PE–backed late-stage startup, was confident he did a good job going through all numbers before committing to the job. His mistake was that his start date was five months after he did his own due diligence and signed the contract.

After he started the CEO role, what he uncovered was not fraud but the fact that some parts of the business materially changed during those five months when he wasn't paying enough attention to day-to-day performance since he was not the CEO yet. An additional challenge was that he didn't delve deeply enough to comprehend the aggressiveness of the business's debt terms. This would materially affect the company's situation later.

However, the consequences were for him to live with. Looking back, Sully wished he had continued to closely monitor what was happening in the business between committing to take over and stepping in as a CEO, and had given a closer look at the company's financing agreements.

Linda, who took over as the CEO of a biotech company, later regretted taking too much information at face value during due diligence. A complex corporate structure gave the impression that the business was cash-positive, which was technically accurate. Still, the reasons for that differed from what Linda assumed without digging deep enough.

Unlike in my business, neither Sully nor Linda were lied to or encountered fraud. Rather, the real situation was not as rosy as they expected. Reflecting on their experience, both of them wished they dug deeper.

Yet not a single founder or professional CEO I interviewed during my research said that they engaged a third party to do due diligence on the business or even took it exceptionally seriously themselves.

Incoming CEOs are sometimes too keen to trust board packs and audited financial statements. In most cases, there will be no unpleasant surprises. However, given that the new CEO will be responsible for fixing whatever mess might come to the surface, it might be prudent to consider borrowing from VC's playbook and conducting a light but formal due diligence process to ensure the new CEO knows what they are signing up for.

LEGAL AND FINANCIAL CONSIDERATIONS

Leaving the company you founded and ran as a CEO is never as straightforward as quitting a regular job. This part of the book is not meant as legal advice but will outline some of the main questions you'll need to consider. For this section, I'm assuming that your business is incorporated in the UK, you are employed in the UK, and you are a UK taxpayer.

In most cases, the legal instrument by which the CEO's employment will be terminated is a settlement agreement. This legal agreement between the company and the CEO sets out the terms on which the CEO is leaving. Generally, it is advisable to enter a settlement agreement regardless of whether the CEO's departure is initiated by them (resignation), by the company (dismissal), or by mutual accord.

A settlement agreement serves several functions. First, it describes the terms of departure: what the departing CEO is paid, what happens to their vested and unvested equity, etc. Second, it comforts the company that the departing employee will not sue. Third, it avoids following a drawn-out formal (and sometimes undignified) dismissal procedure.

A significant advantage of the settlement agreement is that it's final, meaning once it's negotiated and signed, both the company and the CEO have certainty. It draws a line under any potential litigation in case of an acrimonious departure.

When negotiating the settlement agreement, it will be necessary to review various documents, such as the employment agreement of the CEO, the rules of the Employee Share Plan, and the company's constitutional documents (the Shareholders' Agreement and the Articles of Association).

These documents should describe what is expected to happen if the founder leaves the business: for example, how much notice the CEO is entitled to. However, it is only a starting point for the negotiation with the board.

Let's assume that the departing founder doesn't control the board. This means there is a need to negotiate terms that will be acceptable to both sides. Often, the biggest question that must be navigated is what happens to the founder CEO's equity.

Sometimes, the company's documents will have compulsory share transfer provisions, meaning if the founder resigns or is asked to leave, they are required to transfer some or all of their shares back to the company or to other shareholders, often at a "fair market value".

Gretchen Lennon from Lennon Legal, a legal services firm for early-stage businesses that I worked with at Makers, says:

> "One thing to look out for is if the drafting around how the fair market value is calculated: if it is skewed quite heavily in favour of the company, for example, or if it says the fair market value is to be determined by the board acting reasonably.
>
> That gives a huge amount of leeway and prerogative to the board to land at a figure that may not be as generous or fair to the departing CEO as it might have been if determined by independent third-party experts."

In short, the departing founder would be well-advised to understand their legal position thoroughly, get advice from an experienced solicitor, and negotiate a mutually beneficial settlement agreement with the board. This would allow both the company and the founder to feel satisfied that the overall termination package (cash, plus equity, plus any other points of negotiation) is fair and reasonable.

This frees up both the company and the departing CEO to focus on their respective transitions: from departing founder CEO to new CEO (for the company) and from running their own business to doing something new (for the CEO).

Some of the most important clauses in company documents to pay attention to are good and bad leaver provisions. They describe what happens to the founder's equity if they leave the business, depending on when, why and how they leave. There may be more than one set of good and bad leaver provisions, covering the founder's shares and the founder's options, as Gretchen explains:

> "In some cases, there may be two separate sets of good and bad leaver provisions to review. For example, the Articles of Association may contain compulsory transfer provisions for leavers — these may apply to shares held by the departing CEO. In addition, if the CEO also holds options under the company's Employee Share Plan which have not yet been exercised, the leaver provisions in that Plan will apply to those options."

The outgoing CEO must engage a lawyer because the settlement agreement will only be valid if the outgoing employee receives independent legal advice. It is typical for companies to contribute towards the departing employee's lawyer's fees, or the company may even agree to cover these entirely. In any case, the solicitor must be chosen and engaged directly by the founder, not the company itself. The same solicitor can't simultaneously advise the company and the departing founder on the settlement agreement.

The Shareholders' Agreement, Articles of Association and other documents may explicitly set out certain terms applicable to departing employees, or they may provide the board of directors with discretion regarding what happens to the vested and unvested equity. In addition, the board will have discretion regarding how much (if any) money the CEO should be paid as a termination payment. The termination payment and equity treatment are often negotiation points.

For example, the board might ask the founder to stay in the role until a successor is found and appointed (or until a particular event occurs, such as a product launch). In return, the company may offer a more generous termination payment or allow the founder to vest or keep more of their equity.

In addition to the size of the termination payment and the treatment of the CEO's equity, some other questions for consideration are non-compete (are you prevented from working for a competitor or starting a similar company?), non-solicitation (can you hire people who work for the company to work for you?), intellectual property (that side project you were working on, is it yours or the company's?), legal costs (will the company cover some or all of these?), director's loans or personal guarantees (did you lend any money to the company or guarantee any company loans?), anti-embarrassment provisions (these protect you if you miss out on a great exit that happens soon after you leave), personal tax liability (if you have to sell any of your shares back to the company, what are the tax consequences?) and more.

Suppose the founder has agreed to stay on the board or continue working as a consultant/advisor with the company. In that case, the company should prepare a new agreement describing its new relationship with the former CEO. Otherwise, Companies House must be notified if the CEO leaves the board of directors.

As mentioned at the start of the book, founders are not always flush with cash. At the same time, getting a new job after stepping down as a CEO is not always quick, as we'll discuss in the last chapter. However, the CEO will be obliged to focus on the business's success and the transition until the very end of their tenure (without being too distracted with finding a new role or starting their next venture). One of the negotiating factors can thus be the departing CEO's need for cash, influencing whether their termination package is more heavily weighted towards cash rather than equity.

A settlement agreement that offers a tax-efficient cash payout (in the UK, the first £30,000 is income tax-free) to the outgoing CEO allows them to focus more on the business's success, knowing they will have a bit of time and space to figure out their next steps after they step down. Any cash payment over £30,000 will usually be subject to income tax and national insurance contributions.

One non-obvious question that needs to be considered during the transition is whether there are any personal loans lent by the founder to the company or personal guarantees that the founder might have given to the bank or some other creditors in the company's early days (and possibly almost forgotten about, as it was in my case).

In the case of personal loans, it's crucial to include repayment terms in the settlement agreement, especially if they are not documented. Regarding personal guarantees, it is doubtful that the new CEO or any of the investors will be willing to take on the liability for them. However, leaving personal guarantees in place would mean the departing CEO being personally responsible for the actions of new management, over which they will likely have little control.

The best way to address these, therefore, is to negotiate them away with the lender. It may be possible to argue that since they were taken, the business has become stronger and doesn't need those guarantees or can now offer some other security instead. It could also be possible to move to a different lender that won't require personal guarantees from the founder. Since this process will take time, starting these conversations early is best.

There is also a specific issue that the board and the founder might need to discuss, which requires a separate conversation: how to rebalance the cap table.

REBALANCING THE CAP TABLE

As a CEO, I learned that there's no such thing as a fair cap table because everyone's idea of fairness (and their contribution) is different, and often significantly so. It's worth reflecting on some challenges related to the cap table that arise during CEO transitions.

A founder CEO leaving their role usually has a significant equity stake in the business. However, this stake is often called "dead equity" or "dormant equity": equity belonging to people not contributing to the company's growth.

This can be a problem during future fundraising because new investors might think the management is not incentivised enough to grow the business. This can be especially problematic if the cap table already has some dormant equity before the CEO steps down.

According to Nic Brisbourne, these concerns are being raised more and more often by investors and those staying in the business:

> "It's coming up more and more. In investors' minds, dead equity has become much more of an issue during Series A and Series B than it used to be. For some remaining execs, it can be an issue, too.
>
> Some people find it significantly demotivating to think, I'm still killing myself here, whereas someone else has still got similar equity to me but is now earning money elsewhere or enjoying themselves on the beach?"

It's an understandable concern. It can feel unfair for a team member or a remaining co-founder to know that their hard work, year after year, rewards someone who is no longer working in the business.

Dormant equity also reduces the option pool available to incentivise existing and future team members because it can't be used to incentivise the new CEO. In contrast, it was used to incentivise the outgoing CEO. Potential investors would generally expect the share option pool to be maintained at a reasonable level, but enlarging it dilutes all shareholders. This dynamic can make fundraising negotiations difficult.

So, what options are available to the board and the outgoing CEO in this situation?

There are, by and large, two ways to approach it. One is for the founder to transfer or sell some of their equity to the company or an existing investor. The other is to accept dormant equity and issue new share options to incentivise the incoming CEO, diluting all shareholders.

Selling the equity to existing investors can be a win-win for both parties as long as they can agree on the price. Investors who are bullish about the business may be more interested in increasing their stake. If the outgoing CEO is keen to take some cash off the table, they may choose to do it and even accept a discount on the share price to make it more attractive to the investors.

Accepting a discount might be difficult for the outgoing CEO, but it has advantages. As we discussed, startup founders are rarely flush with cash pre-exit, so selling some shares, even at a discount, can give them financial freedom for the coming months, if not years. According to Nic Brisbourne, such secondaries are common:

> "What is quite common is secondaries for founders who left after Series A, Series B, Series C, often at a slight discount to the round price, but usually not a big one."

Another option is for the company to buy back its shares from the outgoing CEO, but this is not always easy. For the company to do it, it must have the cash to buy them. Additionally, it can typically only do it using profits, although some companies find ways around this requirement. So even for well-capitalised but unprofitable startups, buying back shares of the departing CEO may not always be straightforward. Still, according to Gretchen Lennon:

> "Share buybacks for departing founders are quite typical. It's a way for the outgoing founder to cash in on the value of their shares to date. And it is in the company's interests to claw those shares back if it can because this allows the company to use those shares as part of a remuneration package for the new CEO without diluting the shareholding of anyone else."

Yet another option is to ask the outgoing CEO to voluntarily give up some of their shares. This is even harder for the outgoing CEO than accepting a significant discount on a secondary sale. If the Shareholders' Agreement or Articles of Association do not require the CEO to transfer their shares back for little or no value, they get to keep their vested equity.

The only exception to this rule is when they are fired for a cause, and most or all of their vested shares are taken back. Otherwise, giving vested equity up without negotiating something tangible in return would likely be naive. In effect, relinquishing equity is simply a transfer of wealth of the outgoing CEO to remaining shareholders.

Regardless of the mechanics of rebalancing the cap table, the outgoing founder should receive independent legal advice because some aspects of this process may not be apparent. For example, it's quite common for compulsory transfer provisions to say that a company has up to 12 months to buy the departing CEO's shares.

At the same time, if the CEO has share options which they are permitted to exercise when they leave, they may only have 90 days from their termination date to pay the exercise price of these share options. If the company plans to repurchase these shares from the founder within the next 12 months, it may be feasible to offset the exercise price that the founder owes against the amount paid by the company for those shares later on. However, this process requires specialised legal and tax advice.

I heard from some investors (not in my company, thankfully) who believe that when a CEO decides to step down, it should be their responsibility to pay for the new CEO with their equity. This means making a share transfer at a nominal price. According to this logic, since the rest of the shareholders didn't decide that the CEO should step down, they shouldn't be paying for it.

I find this argument misleading and unfair. The purpose of any founder equity vesting mechanism is to reward the work done over a certain period (or in meeting certain milestones). What is vested is vested and fairly earned by the founder. Therefore, unless there's an exceptional case, such as gross misconduct or fraud, they should be entitled to this equity (or at least fair market value for it). It would be no more appropriate to demand any vested equity is given up by the departing CEO than to demand the repayment of salary paid before their departure.

Even more importantly, it's the business that is hiring the new CEO, not the outgoing founder, in a personal capacity. Therefore, it's up to the company to pay for it. I haven't heard of an outgoing CEO being expected to pay the salary of the new one, but somehow, this argument is sometimes applied to equity. In my view, it shouldn't be.

However, it's possible that at some point, a startup might find itself facing an unpalatable choice between running out of cash and raising money from an investor who insists on reducing the amount of dormant equity on the cap table. A departing founder might accept a less favourable deal when choosing between giving up some equity and being left with worthless equity.

If the founder is not transferring some of their shares, this leaves another way forward: enlarging the stock options pool. Dormant equity might be a problem with existing team members or new investors. However, they inevitably see it as a problem not that a departed CEO has "too much" but that they don't have enough given their effort or investment.

Enlarging the stock options pool and allowing the board to make appropriate grants to the new CEO and senior team members at the expense of dilution for all shareholders is often the right thing to do. Yet, it's rarely easy. No one likes being diluted.

Every situation, however, is different and requires careful consideration and sound legal advice. One situation in which giving up some of the shares by an outgoing CEO is the right thing to do might be the case of not having had their shares under a vesting agreement in the first place.

Suppose two co-founders set up a business and subscribed to 50% of shares each without vesting terms. If, say, half a year later, one of them left with 50%, it would be hard to argue that the outgoing co-founder was fairly entitled to walk away with 50% of the company (if anything), and it would be equally challenging to fix it by enlarging the stock option pool.

Institutional investors typically require founders to have vesting schedules as part of the terms of their investments, making such situations increasingly rare.

BUILDING BRIDGES WITH THE SENIOR MANAGEMENT TEAM

While the senior management team (SMT) will not be as involved in selecting and appointing the new CEO as the founders and the board, the change will undoubtedly impact them.

The SMT will know about the CEO succession earlier, possibly much earlier, than the rest of the team because they will need to be involved in preparing it. They might also recognise tell-tale signs of the board preparing for the CEO change.

The best way to address it is for the new CEO to be open and upfront about their plans wherever possible. It might be helpful to reinforce the commitment to the existing strategy or outline the contours of a new one. The incoming CEO, yet to be formally appointed, might choose to communicate their priorities privately to the SMT.

While the CEO will have the top title, they won't get anything done without winning the hearts and minds of the rest of the business, starting with their direct reports. Claudia explained it later:

> "I think one of the things that helped me to be successful in this transition is early wins. I'm a great believer that the title of the CEO conveys no power on you. In some ways, I was lucky to take over during a slight crisis because I could convincingly get the business back onto its feet in the post-COVID era. You're not along for the ride; you're almost immediately a builder. And that's been very important."

Setting expectations and getting early wins will show the senior team what working with the new CEO will be like.

They say that there's only one opportunity to make the first impression. If the new CEO is an insider — a co-founder or another senior management team member — they can make the first impression again, this time as a CEO.

BREAKING THE NEWS TO THE WORLD

As discussed earlier in the book, it's best to share the news of the transition with the entire team and the world when there is clarity on how it will work.

You'll need to consider several audiences: investors, senior management, wider team, clients, media, the industry, regulatory bodies, key partners and anyone you were a key contact for.

In this section, I assume that the new CEO joining your business to replace you has been headhunted from another CEO position. Hence, the transition must be communicated on both sides: their old company and your startup.

The communication process must be tightly orchestrated because every team must hear the news from their CEO, not from the other company that makes the announcement first.

This can amount to substantial activity across different channels, even for a small startup. Hence, it's worth planning it carefully. Here's one way in which it could be done, which you might choose to adapt to your circumstances.

Once you know when the new CEO is taking over, this needs to be communicated in confidence to the senior management teams of both companies.

As we discussed in the previous chapter, the SMT will have questions about what it means for them, and it would be wise for the new CEO to be ready to listen to the senior team and offer answers to any questions they may have. A successful outcome of this step is a senior management team that understands what is happening, why it's happening, what it means for them and their work going forward.

In particular, the senior team will start preparing to support their teams when the news breaks. Everyone on the team will have questions about what it means for them and the business, which they will raise in one-to-ones with their managers, so the senior team must be ready to answer their questions.

Next, the relevant person on the senior management teams of both companies, for example, Head of Marketing or Chief of Staff, is tasked with preparing a communication plan, deciding how to notify every audience and preparing draft messages for blogs, emails and social media. A successful outcome is a detailed, written communication plan agreed upon by both CEOs. It's easy to forget someone on the day. A thorough plan prevents this from happening.

Choose a day when it's possible to have all-hands meetings one after another at both companies. A virtual town hall will work well if both companies welcome hybrid working.

These meetings are an opportunity for the outgoing CEO to explain why they are stepping down and introduce the new CEO, who can explain how excited they are to take over and what it means for the business.

The rest of the communications plan will be executed as soon as these two meetings are over. Pre-written articles will be posted on the company blog and social media channels. At the same time, those contacts you choose to notify directly will receive personalised emails or phone calls if your relationship has been particularly close.

Just like with the team, your clients and suppliers will wonder what the leadership change means for them. Will you continue to be a reliable partner for them? Will you continue to be an important client? Will you be able to introduce them to the new CEO? Thinking through the questions and explaining the reasons for the change and its implications will help maintain the relationships.

One group that's easy to overlook is new employees who have already signed the contract but haven't started the job yet or are in the late stages of the interviewing process. It may be helpful for their future manager to give them a quick call to explain that the company is still very excited about their joining and that there's no reason to believe that their offer might be under threat.

While, in all likelihood, the CEO transition won't affect new joiners, it would be a shame to lose a great new employee only because they incorrectly assume that the change of leadership means they should not join your company. Sometimes, a little reassurance goes a long way.

Another group that's easy to overlook are people who aren't in the office that day because of a planned holiday, illness or a day off. While it's undoubtedly best practice not to contact people who are "out of the office" unless it's an emergency, a change of the CEO warrants it: it's best to hear about the news from their manager or the outgoing CEO themselves than from a mention on social media.

If you have a large number of small angel investors who don't have information rights and don't play any role in the company's life, you must decide whether to notify them while sharing the news with the senior team or with the entire world. Telling them before you tell the senior team increases the risk of a leak and is best avoided.

It's probably best not to plan urgent work on the announcement day in case you need to be available for any follow-up conversations. However, compared to other aspects of navigating the CEO transition in startups, communicating the change is one of the easiest aspects of it.

SAYING GOODBYES

On my way out as a CEO, my time was split between two activities: preparing the handover and saying goodbye to the team.

At first, I didn't plan to say individual goodbyes, but once it occurred to me, I offered everyone on the team to book half an hour with me, and nearly everyone did. I fondly remember many of these conversations.

Rituals matter. When we get married, we don't simply sign the paperwork. We mark the occasion. When Christmas comes, we buy presents and watch old holiday movies (okay, maybe just me). Whenever there's a significant change in our lives or in the life of a community, it's essential to find a way to talk about it, reflect on its meaning, and acknowledge what's happening.

Every conversation with my colleagues was different. With some early team members, we laughed as we reminisced about the early days of the business when there were just half a dozen of us, pizza-fuelled twenty-somethings, building a new startup. With others, I was asked why I was stepping down—and I, at times, chose to be slightly more open in private conversations than I was in my public announcement.

Yet others asked me about the new CEO and what to expect from her. They might have felt the business was losing its startup flair and was becoming "more corporate." It was an opportunity for me to acknowledge such sentiment and explain that maybe it was time for some of our "startup flair" to go.

Above all, these final one-to-ones gave me a chance to reassure the team, one by one, that things were okay and that while CEO transitions can be unsettling, this one was going well. I'll never really know, but I like to think that expressing, privately and sincerely, my support for the new CEO helped the team embrace the leadership change without undue worry.

On my side, these conversations were also a bit therapeutic. I was going through a transition period myself. While my main focus was to ensure that the business would be okay after I left, I also started to realise that in just a few days, I would set up an auto-responder on my work email, sign off from Slack, and wake up on a working day without any meetings to attend. My small ritual to mark the transition was saying goodbye to everyone on the team individually.

Congratulations, you have reached a significant milestone in your CEO transition! Most of the work is behind you now. You decided to step down, found a great successor, and orchestrated a smooth transition.

As we have seen, the most crucial aspect of this stage is getting out of the way of the new CEO. You hired them for a reason. Now, it's time to give them all the freedom they need. They know where to find you.

It's also essential to get out of the way to find mental space to focus on what's next for you. As we'll discuss in the next chapter, this moment in your career is truly special. One chapter is over, and another hasn't started yet. It's worth approaching this moment with deliberation and care.

Questions to reflect on:

- What do you need to do or let go of to allow the new CEO to assume full leadership?
- What measures can you implement to ensure the business is stable?
- How can you support your senior team and staff during this transition period?
- What are the key legal considerations that need to be addressed before your departure?
- How will you bid farewell to the team in a way that honours your time together?

CHAPTER 8

REST AND REFLECT ON YOUR CAREER OPTIONS

Rest and reflection are indispensable skills in life because they bring clarity to the direction of travel and energy to keep going. Now that you are no longer running your business, what's next for you?

Before you answer this question, it's important to slow down, rest and reflect. You've been running fast for a long time. This is a perfect moment in your life to reflect on how you feel after running your startup for many years, what matters to you and what you want to do next. And, maybe, meet some of the fears as your old friends.

In the following chapter, we will examine various career paths that founder CEOs tend to follow after they step down, but first, let's talk about how to get the break you need and deserve.

WHAT'S NEXT FOR YOU?

The transition doesn't end when the new CEO officially takes the title, and the old CEO gives it up. Life goes on. This chapter of your life might be over, but a new one has just begun. What's next for you after you step down as a CEO, having run your startup for many years?

This question is essential, and it rarely has an obvious answer. It's essential because this moment is a rare opportunity to take your career in a different direction, should you wish so. You have valuable experience, a robust professional network, a deep understanding of your industry, and the freedom to make the next move. Good moments to change our career trajectory don't come often because to get good at something, we must spend many years doing it.

The first such moment comes in our youth when we choose our first job or a university degree, but then we don't yet have the lived experience and rarely have the self-awareness to know what path to take. Changing a career after you've spent only a few years working in a given field or job will probably set you back as you haven't had a chance to gain enough experience or establish yourself in that field.

However, stepping down as a startup CEO, assuming you ran your business for a meaningful amount of time and achieved a degree of success, gives you a personal and professional platform from which you can pivot to something new without losing the progress you've made in your career.

It's like a career "save point" in a video game, where you can go in a different direction, but you still have all the achievements, experience and self-awareness you've gained. Many people have such moments only once or twice in their careers, so it makes sense to use this opportunity wisely.

However, regardless of what you choose to do next, I bet you need some good rest, even if you haven't realised it yet.

BEFORE ANYTHING ELSE, YOU NEED A BREAK

A client of mine, Øyvind Reed, founder and CEO of Whereby, stepped down after more than a decade of running his startup, which is now led by one of his executives. Considering his next steps, Øyvind admitted that his biggest risk was jumping into something new without reflecting and recovering. The habit and inertia of being constantly busy, productive and surrounded by people can be a powerful force, pulling us back into a familiar environment.

The constant busyness of running a startup often prevents us from realising how tired we are. We might be so used to masking how we feel by being busy, caffeinated, and focused on the next big goal that we may even start forgetting what it's like to feel how we are in the present moment.

As founder CEOs, we are often focused on optimising our time. We want to know whether we're working on the most important thing most efficiently. Our sense of identity merges with the business we founded. We may feel guilty spending time on anything other than the business, including health, family and friends.

Tom Savage, a British serial entrepreneur, describes his experience:

> "The moment you take away the responsibilities of being a CEO, with the accompanying adrenal fuel, you realise quite how stressed you were. I look at others running the show and wonder how I lasted so long. I feel, for the first time in a long time, like I have space in my life to meander, to talk to people in the street, to engage in relationships without feeling like I should probably head back to my desk to forge on."

Every startup founder I know who stepped down as a CEO recommends taking time to rest, reflect and plan the next steps after stepping down. How long? Longer than you think you need. If you've spent years running a startup, you're probably used to taking no more than two weeks off for a holiday. However, whatever the correct answer is in your circumstances, it's probably measured in months or even years, not weeks.

At first, you might feel the freedom — and maybe terror — of not having anything scheduled for the day and not watching every hour of your time. If you let yourself rest for a few weeks, you may become more aware of your exhaustion and feel itchy to jump back into action to avoid this discomfort.

You will meet some of your fears. Maybe an inner voice says that your next act won't live up to the success your business has enjoyed so far. Or, maybe you'll fear losing status in your professional community if you're in between two stages for too long. These fears will also make it tempting to distract yourself with work.

If you resist these temptations and think systematically about what's next, eventually, you'll find yourself in a place where you feel rested, clear about what you want to do next and energised to go for it.

For me, this rest period coincided with moving from London to Portugal and exploring what it's like to work remotely. Instead of jumping back into action, I gradually eased into it by first starting training as a coach, which I had long planned to do. I then started coaching my first clients part-time, progressively increasing my workload as I became more confident that it was the right next professional step for me.

For James Routledge, this time was spent working through his sense of guilt and doubt:

> "I felt guilty that I had not seen the business through. I felt guilty towards the team I'd left behind that might be having a hard time. And I had some genuine feelings of doubt: Wait, was this the right call? Have I made the wrong decision here? Have I fucked this up? Have I thrown away a good thing? Am I just sitting around on a beach instead?
>
> There were moments of peace, but also, at times, I was quite hard on myself. And then some moments of, Okay, this is why I did this.
>
> Now I can ask questions I wasn't asking before because of the space I've afforded myself."

I've yet to meet a single founder CEO who leaves their business after running it for years and is bursting with energy, ready to tackle a new challenge. Any intense job that involves long hours, stress, responsibility, and risks will take its toll unless we learn to make it truly sustainable, which—as I know from working with my founder clients and from my personal experience—is easier said than done.

So, if you can afford it, allow time off after stepping down. It's essential to face your feelings and be mentally prepared for the challenges ahead instead of keeping yourself busy to avoid them.

You don't have to leave your business to take a meaningful break. Adam Fudakowski, the founder who stepped down as the CEO of Switchee to join its senior management team, took three months off after leaving his CEO job. This break gave him time and space to recover while giving the new CEO time and space to make the role his own without feeling like the previous CEO was watching over his shoulder.

In hindsight, this choice made perfect sense for Adam, the new CEO and the business. Still, reflecting on it later, Adam admitted that he didn't even consider the possibility of asking the board for a paid three-month sabbatical, having been so committed to the business for many years, until the new CEO suggested it.

Regardless of how long your break is, there are two big jobs you need to do during this period of transition. First, give yourself physical and mental rest. Second, think through what you want to focus on next.

TAKING A WELL-DESERVED REST

Reflecting on how he felt after stepping down, Øyvind said:

> "I started to feel my body again. When you used to ask me what sensations I noticed in my chest, in my legs, and my arms, I used not to know how to answer this question. I was always in my head. Now I am starting to feel my body again."

In our coaching conversations, we started talking less about managing his relationships with the board and more about being fully present with his family on holidays after years of being glued to his work inbox at all times.

A warning sign that you may need some deep rest is an inability to stay still and do nothing for a while. By doing nothing, I don't mean watching Netflix and then going clubbing with friends, but enjoying slow, quality time in nature or meditation, in the presence of your thoughts and feelings and without trying to distract yourself.

It can be difficult. We spent so many years working on the business, thinking about the business, thinking about ourselves as the founder and CEO of our business, that not doing it can feel like looking into a bottomless abyss. It's okay to be disoriented as we learn to reconnect with ourselves and discover who we are when we are not running a company.

This recovery process can take time, reflection and deep conversations with others who've been there. We can't know how long it will take, but the promise is that we'll start rediscovering ourselves and getting comfortable in our own skin. An even more significant promise is that our career decisions will be based on a deeper understanding of our desires. This will allow us to make informed decisions about how we want to spend the next decade and even the rest of our lives.

A sign of deep rest is inner peace that we enjoy when we can just be without doing anything or going anywhere. This inner peace is the foundation for freedom because when we are not compelled to do this or that, we are free to choose what to do. This allows us to face our thoughts and feelings, even when challenging. Then, we can choose what to do next in our career from a place of strength and self-awareness.

Rest doesn't come easy if our minds and bodies are used to the fast pace of a startup environment. There are two common traps to fall into. One is to continue doing what's familiar: reading industry news, networking with other entrepreneurs or joining panels at events — things you never had enough time for as CEO but which are familiar to you.

Another is to drift off into sloth and torpor, watching Netflix in the morning and then wandering around the golf course, wondering why it feels empty inside when you're having a drink at 4 pm.

Either would be a mistake. Rest may be the opposite of work, but it would benefit from discipline and a structured approach. It's easy to imagine that once we are not running our startup, we'll finally have time to exercise, learn a new foreign language, travel to see our friends and go on a meditation retreat. The truth is that unless we plan what we want to do and how we want to do it, we risk slipping either into what's familiar or what's easy.

So, how would you like to rest? What is most important to you about this period of your life? How would you like to balance health, learning, self-care and pursuing dreams you never had time for?

What would you like your self-care routine to look like? What things like meditation or tennis have you always wanted to learn but never had time for? What books have you wished you had time to read? How much screen time would you like to have per day?

Schedule things. You ran a startup for years, so you are skilled at setting goals, reflecting on desired outcomes and following your calendar. Use your professional habits to apply them to this period of your life. As founders and CEOs, we set goals, execute strategies and reevaluate them based on the results. The same approach can be applied to rest.

For example, I needed to enjoy a daily outdoor activity, such as a long walk, something I didn't always have time for as a founder. I also started training as a coach and soon began working with my first clients.

Øyvind started a big DIY project at home, rediscovered his passion for sports and spent more quality time with his kids than he ever did as a CEO.

One thing we don't always prioritise when running our companies is relationships. What would it be like to spend more time and be present with our children and our partners? When was the last time we visited our parents and had as much time as necessary to listen to their stories? When did we last take time to take our nephew for an afternoon in a theme park? Would some of our friendships benefit from late-night conversations or weekends away?

The reason to ask ourselves all these questions isn't just to allow ourselves to enjoy and strengthen our relationships but also to discover who we are. Our identities, the way we experience ourselves, are shaped by what we do and who we spend our time with.

Our sense of self is deeply relational. I challenge you to say anything about who you are without referring to something external: founder of a company, citizen of a country, expert in some field, fan of something or someone, parent of a child, partner of someone else. We define and experience ourselves as a reflection of our activities and relationships.

Navigating the transition as a CEO can benefit greatly from being immersed in old and new relationships and making new experiences. It allows us to discover more about ourselves and our values, informing our next steps.

When we step down as a founder CEO after a decade of running our business, we may feel that running a startup is the only path forward we can see. The intensity of our experience limits our sense of identity and possibility. Allowing ourselves to rest and proactively taking steps to reignite our relationships and expose ourselves to new experiences can be a mirror in which we may better see who we are and what's next for us.

What are some of the big things that you never had time for? Have you ever dreamed of walking the Camino de Santiago de Compostela in Spain with other pilgrims? Or riding your motorcycle across a continent? Or dedicating a lot of your time and energy to helping a charity? Or taking an extended meditation retreat? Or taking your family on an incredible adventure you always said you'd do one day? Or maybe taking a sabbatical to write a sitcom script?

However you decide to rest, my invitation is to deliberate about it. Resist the temptation to jump into something familiar, like accepting the first decent job offer. Resist the temptation to do what's easy because you might not notice how this incredibly precious period of your life might slip through your fingers. Approach it with care, positive intentions and a sense of gratitude that you can stop and ground yourself while thinking about what's next.

REFLECTING ON WHAT YOU VALUE

As we discussed above, leaving your startup after running it for many years is a significant transition point that offers an opportunity to choose the next step in your career.

Our experience, skills, and professional networks offer an enviable choice of opportunities. But we need to start not with what's available but with who we are and what we want.

I often ask my coaching clients about their idea of a good life. Many, or even most, are surprised by this question, admitting they haven't thought deeply about it. Yet, how can we live a good life if we can't articulate our aim? Of course, our idea of a good life will constantly change throughout life, which is healthy and shows that we are growing and evolving. However, not thinking about it leaves us at the mercy of following social conventions and our unexamined assumptions.

My idea of living a good life involves helping others, having meaningful relationships and deep conversations, being close to nature, simplicity, and peace of mind. It also means having a positive impact on the world and on the people that I know.

I believe that nothing in our life is an accident, but not in the sense that everything's predetermined. Instead, everything happens for a reason, and we can and should look back at our lives to learn from what happened to discover patterns and valuable lessons.

Looking back, it's clear that I started Makers primarily out of a sense of insecurity, aiming to prove myself and win imaginary approval from others by building something valuable. But it also became clear that what kept me at Makers was a sense that it was an opportunity to help our students change their lives.

In our first year, before I stepped up to take up the CEO role when my cofounder Rob left, I coached students myself to become software developers. I saw them go from writing their first line of code to signing their first employment contract within months. Only in retrospect did I appreciate how meaningful that direct, personal connection was to me.

Likewise, looking back, it was clear that once the business started to grow and my focus inevitably shifted from working with students to working with numbers and strategy, I drifted further away from my idea of a good life.

For years, I tried to trick myself into thinking that I must have been living my dream life because my work impacted plenty of students as we kept changing more and more lives at Makers. This was objectively true, but at my heart, I knew that I was not living my idea of a good life. Now I understand that my one and only depressive episode when I was a CEO was there to shake me awake and remind me that something needed to change.

In hindsight, it's not a surprise that what helped me better understand myself were my founder coaches with whom I worked over the years as a CEO. Session after session, year after year, they helped me go inside, reflecting on the questions that wouldn't go away.

Who am I? What have I learned about myself in my life so far? What are my strengths and weaknesses? What skills do I bring to the table? What do I value? What gives me energy, and what drains me? What do I value most, as evidenced by my actions, not my words? What were the real, deep reasons for starting this business? What are my hopes and dreams? What are my fears?

Jerry Colonna, the coach who led CEO Bootcamp, a five-day immersive programme for startup founders in Colorado that I attended in 2015, shared a Buddhist tale of Milarepa with us, 14 startup CEOs, sitting in a circle around a fireplace on a crisp winter day.

According to legend, Milarepa lived and meditated in a remote cave. One day, he returned to the cave only to find it filled with scary demons. They were flying around, big and small, all noisy and unpleasant to look at.

Keen to meditate in peace, Milarepa tried to throw them out, running after them, shouting at them. But the demons wouldn't leave. It even seemed that new ones started to join them.

Realising the futility of his efforts, Milarepa decided to teach them Buddhist wisdom. The demons started paying attention and quieted down but didn't leave.

Taking a deep breath, Milarepa asked them instead, "What are you ready to teach me?" One after another, the demons began sharing their teachings with Milarepa, and once they were satisfied that he had understood them, they departed from the cave.

Yet, one demon stayed in the cave. It was the largest, scariest demon that Milarepa was afraid to even look at. Realising he was powerless against this demon, Milarepa went to him and put his head into his ugly mouth, saying, "Eat me if you wish."

At this moment, the demon disappeared.

For years, I was afraid to face the demon within me. This demon was the realisation that my career path was leading me away from something deeply important to me. It also made me wonder if the business would be off with another CEO.

In his book *Reboot: Leadership and The Art of Growing Up*, written for founders on the journey of self-discovery, Jerry writes about facing his demon, acknowledging that he wasn't and didn't need to be as rich as Bill Gates.

> "I wasn't and—importantly, had no need to be—Bill Gates. Indeed, I often think of the teaching of Jesus. It's a lesser-known teaching from one of the Gnostic Gospels, the Gospel of Saint Thomas:
>
> 'If you bring forth what is in you, what is in you will save you. If you do not bring forth what is in you, what is in you will destroy you.'
>
> Jesus taught a truth: the only choice that doesn't destroy you is to bring forth who you were meant to be. The

> alchemy of becoming yourself is the ultimate magic act and fullest expression of leadership.
>
> In all these thoughts I read a steady, consistent wisdom: the wisdom of knowing yourself and your own beliefs and living them. Enduring the alchemical crucible requires developing the capacity to reflect, to turn the pain of the everyday life as a leader into lessons. Every wisdom tradition I've ever encountered demands the same thing: we must go inward."

My own way of saying "Eat me if you wish" was the decision to take action: start looking for a new CEO at Makers and start a new career for myself before I knew how it would all turn out.

Going inwards, reflecting on my own beliefs, whether I lived or betrayed them, and exploring who I am meant to be helped me realise a simple truth: I thrive when I can make a difference in someone's life through a deep, meaningful connection.

Looking at what it means in practice brought me time and time again to the idea of training as a coach myself. The simplicity and joy of helping other leaders become themselves and live a life aligned with their inner truth brought forth another big demon: What if I'm not going to be a good coach?

That's the demon I've been courting since I started coaching others. My way of putting my head into its salivating mouth is admitting that I am not a perfect coach. I've plenty to learn. I make mistakes.

And yet, I am walking my path, waking up every morning aiming to bring forth who I am meant to be, living it through mistakes and successes, wins and losses, remembering that if I want to be a good coach by the time I'm fifty, I did well by starting this journey before I was forty.

My way of putting my head in the demon's mouth is putting trust in my sense of who I am and what work I am meant to be doing instead of hoping that achieving a certain goal or making a certain amount of money will constitute a life well lived.

While there's no easy framework for thinking about what's next for you, it is imperative to reflect deeply on what matters to you and why since it will inform your next steps. The opportunity you have now is to take your career in a new direction, building it on the foundation of your business experience, connections and self-awareness acquired on your founder journey.

By this point, you likely have a good idea of your next professional step. In the next, final chapter, we'll examine seven different career paths that founder CEOs often pursue after they step down.

Questions to reflect on:

- How can you plan rest and recovery to make it rejuvenating and fulfilling?
- What defines a fulfilling and meaningful life for you?
- What personal challenges, fears, or limiting beliefs must you confront?
- Reflecting on your transition, what have you learned about what truly motivates you?
- How can you redefine success for yourself, moving beyond conventional ideas?

CHAPTER 9

CHOOSE YOUR NEXT PROFESSIONAL STEP

As founders, we are better placed than many to find our vocation, an occupation that will bring us closer to what we feel deep inside we should be doing. Our skills, connections and experiences give us a wide choice of professional paths we can take.

Taking the time to rest and reflect will give you the clarity you need to choose the next professional step. The answer doesn't have to be final. In fact, it can't be final because every stage of our career inevitably ends, and then we enter a new period of transition.

In this final chapter, we will look at seven career choices founders tend to make after leaving their startups. None of them is right or wrong, but some will resonate with you more than others.

JOINING THE SENIOR MANAGEMENT TEAM

Stepping down to join the management team at your own business under the leadership of a new CEO doesn't happen nearly as often as it could, given how much sense it makes in some situations.

In a growing startup, the founder CEO gets further away from their functional skills. Suppose they have a technical background and have built the first version of their SaaS product. They have appointed a tech lead to run the tech team but are avoiding hiring a CTO because they hesitate to delegate top-level technical decisions to someone else.

In this situation, as the business grows, this founder will have a choice between focusing on their CEO role, letting go of their technical responsibilities, and stepping down as a CEO to focus on leading the tech function as a CTO.

These are two very different career tracks, suitable for different individuals and requiring different skill sets. Theoretically, this should be an easy choice for someone who sees themselves growing as a CTO but needs help with the CEO skill set. In practice, this is rare.

A perceived loss of status can play a role. As social animals, we are deeply aware of how others perceive us. It takes self-awareness and humility to realise that having a business card with the top title when our talents can be better applied in a different role is simply an ego's attempt to feel better about itself.

Our ego can be thought of as a set of strategies we came up with to protect ourselves from the pain we once felt. It's not something terrible to remove or escape; it's simply a mechanism by which our minds operate. Quite often, it's useful, which is why evolution favours it.

However, sometimes, it can get too protective because it imagines the threat is too significant, and social status is one area where our egos sometimes go into overdrive.

From an evolutionary standpoint, it makes sense: for most of our history, loss of status was linked to a threat to well-being or life. However, in modern society, we don't face the same challenges we used to face living in tribes, but our brains have remained essentially unchanged since that time. That's why our egos sometimes overreact to a perceived loss of status.

Likewise, our egos may overreact to the idea that someone else can do the job better than we can. While entirely understandable, there are two scenarios where stepping down as a founder CEO of your startup to remain on the senior team can be a great move.

The first scenario is a founder CEO growing a successful startup, showing promising results and learning on the job. The business has already found product-market fit; it has raised Series A or B and is successfully navigating scaling challenges. The board and the founders can all sense the significant opportunity in front of them. Why step down?

If, at this point, you sense that an experienced scale-up CEO would do a better job faster, but you are still committed to the business and want to be part of the story, a move to a senior position may be a true win-win. This is especially true if you feel exhausted after years of hard work or if learning the scale-up CEO skill set doesn't excite you.

It's tempting to focus on what's best for us. A better question is what's best for the business overall because if the business is booming, there will be enough fun, money and opportunities for everyone involved.

The real question is how to make the company successful, not what job you'll have there. If stepping down to join the SMT will help your business become a rocket ship, that's a win-win. Furthermore, you can carve out a perfect role for yourself in this scenario.

Adam Fudakowski, a serial entrepreneur from the UK whom we met earlier in the book, only saw himself staying in his CEO role for a while. When his business Switchee demonstrated evidence of reaching product-market fit, he was already thinking about his successor. Having found a perfect candidate who spent a few months in a Head of Strategy role before being promoted to CEO, Adam joined the senior team focusing on M&A opportunities and international expansion.

This move put Adam in a strong position. The new CEO did a great job after Adam stepped down. Stepping down also allowed Adam to do what he's good at while he was planning his next move, having started two businesses so far:

> "Over my lifetime, I want to start five businesses. I really like the early stage. And once I've seen a business through that early stage, other people are better at making that scaling journey."

This is a win-win scenario for both Adam and the business. The business retained his expertise while being led by a new, experienced scale-up CEO. Adam is doing what he's good at while having the option to make his next move at any time.

The second scenario in which it makes sense to join the senior team is the CEO running an early-stage company that has made significant progress, e.g. in scientific research but hasn't found a repeatable and scalable business model yet.

If the founder CEO does not have the skills necessary to get the business to the point when it's ready to start scaling its operations, but they can see themselves being a leader of their functional area as the company grows, stepping down to the senior level can be the best move.

However, as discussed earlier, replacing a founder CEO before product-market fit is hard. In practice, such a CEO transition is more likely to succeed when passed from one co-founder to another, minimising disruption.

In both cases, it is essential that the founder CEO sincerely embraces the new role and doesn't try to undermine the new CEO. As I argued in previous chapters, you shouldn't have stepped down if you wanted to keep running your business. And if you did, your job is to support the new CEO.

STARTING A NEW BUSINESS

Tom Savage argues that some of us are "founders, not CEOs". Some are far better at identifying promising ideas and finding repeatable and scalable business models than building solid businesses around them.

The best definition of a startup I've ever seen is by Steve Blank: "A startup is an organization formed to search for a repeatable and scalable business model." One way to think about the CEO's job is building a successful business around that repeatable and scalable business model once it's found.

It's essential to identify which skill set you want to develop to achieve business success and maintain your sanity: searching for a repeatable and scalable business model or building a business around it.

I'm thinking of a founder who'll remain anonymous, whose company produced several innovative products well-received by early adopters and recognised by the industry. However, the founder CEO is far better at developing new product ideas, and the team is far better at building excellent prototypes than making a large, scalable, profitable business. For this founder, the next step in their career, should they decide to hire someone to replace them, will almost certainly be starting a new business.

That could be a wise move. Most importantly, the founder will be far better aligned with who they are and what kind of work they want to do, while the business will get the CEO it needs to address operational challenges and scale.

This founder will also diversify their entrepreneurial portfolio, potentially giving themselves more chances to achieve significant financial success without putting all eggs in one basket, as many entrepreneurs tend to do.

Sometimes, starting a new business can be a mistake. Sully, who took over from a founder CEO in his previous company and led it to an impressive exit, demonstrated his skill set as a CEO but then decided to start a new business instead.

Two years later, he summarised his experiments exploring different business ideas with a simple lesson: "Being a CEO and being a founder are two completely different jobs. I'm good at only one of them." This realisation led him to accept another CEO job at a late-stage PE-backed startup instead of starting another business.

For many founder CEOs stepping down or being fired from their startups by their boards, starting another company can be an excellent move because it leverages their skill set and professional network. Raising money again for a new venture can be easier than raising it the very first time, especially if the previous company made good progress.

However, the success of this move depends on the quality of the inner work the founder did before leaving their previous business. We will repeat the same mistakes if we misunderstand why we chose to leave our startup. Life will teach us the same lessons until we learn them.

That's why realising that we are, for example, a stereotypical "founder, not CEO" can be an excellent reason to start another business. At the same time, leaving the company because, for example, we struggle to deal with stress or have a poor relationship with key people there may well be hiding a deeper problem.

If we're hoping to be more successful or more fulfilled with a new product and a new set of co-founders or investors, we may be looking at the wrong problem to fix. There's a risk that we're mistaken in thinking that the grass is greener on the other side.

However, it could also be a good move. Some startups make mistakes at an early stage that are next to impossible to fix later. It's like having a crack at the foundation: no matter what you do with the building on top, the crack will still be there.

When I was first raising investment, I had no experience of doing it. Yet I was facing professional investors who negotiated such deals for a living. While the company's brilliant lawyer, Chris Grew from Orrick, helped me negotiate away the most damaging clauses, the resulting capitalisation table favoured the investors and early advisors too much while not having enough equity for the early hires who later drove most of the value creation.

The resulting cap table didn't kill the business or cause me to leave, but it taught me a valuable lesson: some mistakes made at the very start can be hard or impossible to fix.

A founder of an AI company, let's call him Richard, learned the same lesson in different circumstances. With the benefit of hindsight, his mistake was to commit to starting the business with the wrong co-founder. While there are always two sides to every story, it's fair to say that the breakdown in their working relationship proved to be far more challenging to navigate than the technical or commercial challenges they faced.

If starting a business with the wrong co-founder or making other hard-to-fix mistakes early on led to the founder leaving the company, starting another startup might be the right next step.

GETTING A CORPORATE JOB

Ilana Lever co-founded Motley, which aimed to provide consumers with access to affordable jewellery based on creations by world-class designers, after spending the early years of her career at a large consultancy, just like several of her friends from university. Despite some challenges with working for a large organisation, Ilana liked her experience as a consultant and working in-house, which gave her the connections, skills and confidence to start her startup in her twenties and raise venture capital.

Several years later, it was time for Ilana and her co-founder to acknowledge that their startup wouldn't work on a venture scale despite all their progress thanks to their blood, sweat and tears. Ilana was understandably exhausted by this point and looking for something more stable than an early-stage startup. Going back into consulting was the most obvious option for Ilana.

> "Popular wisdom is to take time, reflect, and know what you want to do. And I think sometimes that ignores the reality of life. I just got a mortgage and knew I had to get a job."

As she was interviewing, Ilana noticed plenty of emotions coming up. As founders, we often feel our identity fused with our startup. Working for a big corporation might feel alien, even if it makes intellectual sense. We might think the only way to work is to be guided by a passion for our ideas.

For a while, Ilana was looking for a way to reconcile her experience of building a startup she was passionate about and the prospect of working for a monthly paycheque.

The transition to the corporate world may also be hard for our peers to understand, making us feel like we don't belong in the entrepreneurial community. This is misguided. Other founders might empathise with our transition experience much better than our friends and family if they've never been entrepreneurs.

These feelings are real, and yet not many people talk about them openly, including on LinkedIn, the go-to place for feigned vulnerability these days:

> "I think there is an expectation that you will go on and found another business. And the placing of that expectation can make one feel lesser. I felt lesser and embarrassed to be going into a corporate job.
>
> I don't think people talk about shame. And they don't talk about sadness, and they don't talk about lack of confidence. Often, I find on LinkedIn that even the negative stories have a positive spin."

Speaking to her contacts at large companies like the one she used to work for, Ilana realised that the corporate world could sometimes struggle to put her into a box, leading them to discount her startup experience.

Never mind that she raised funding, hired people, led teams, solved complex problems and demonstrated remarkable tenacity, resourcefulness and leadership skills. From the perspective of some larger companies, Ilana looked like a jack of all trades, master of none.

This situation presented a problem for Ilana. The big consultancies were only willing to have a conversation about restarting her career at the seniority level she had when she left to start her startup many years ago. From their perspective, her startup wasn't big enough to consider her for a C-suite role, and she didn't have the technical expertise to qualify for jobs one level below C-suite in the hierarchy.

By discounting her skills and experience, large consultancies offered Ilana far less money than she would have made had she stayed on a corporate career track. Seeing her university friends who never started a startup several levels up the corporate ladder didn't help.

Ilana interviewed extensively and got rejected a lot. However, her tenacity paid off. Ilana found a position at Ocado, a leading grocery technology business better suited for her background and goals. Although that role was at a more junior level than she expected, she was promoted within months of joining.

Her experience exemplifies the challenge that startup founders face when trying to get a job in the corporate world after leaving their startup: not only might they be navigating complex feelings, but they might struggle to find the language to present their professional experience.

This is different from not being qualified for the job. In theory, thanks to their experience of successfully navigating the chaos and challenges of startup life, founders should have the skills prized by employers, large and small. In practice, these employers often can't read the founder's resume, as if it were written in a foreign language they don't speak. An HR department rarely has an insight into what a startup founder can accomplish.

On top of this, startup founders looking for their next job might not have the experience of applying for jobs or interviewing. They know how to sell their businesses but not their skills in an interview. They might have interviewed thousands of people at their own business, but the last time they sat on the other side of the table might have been a decade ago — or never.

As a result, founder after founder describing their attempts to get a job in the corporate world after leaving their startup chooses the same words: "I feel I'm unemployable."

The real picture is more complex. Founders joining the corporate world have a wealth of experience to bring once they find their way in and find a way to fit in. Monica, a founder who sold her startup to a big insurer, learned that the acquirer's board was more interested in her and her team than their technology.

The board of this multi-billion pound company realised they needed to innovate to stay relevant and hoped that Monica could help them. At first, Monica was excited about the opportunity, but she quickly realised how different this bureaucracy was from the startup world she knew:

> "I felt like my role there was less to innovate, but more to educate them: 'This is not the way that you build new products. It's not the way to get new ideas out to market. We can't spend all the time in discussions; we need to actually put things on the market and test them.' In the startup world, you just do that. It was just such a wake-up call.

> They spent very little time talking about the customer. It was always about what's best for the organisation, what fits our process. It was always process-first, although they would never admit that. They're not given the decision-making capability. They're not given ownership. And so it's always like, 'Oh, we need to invite five more people to the call and have another call to talk about the next call.'"

However, it was not the bureaucracy that finally persuaded Monica to leave. It was how she felt about the business:

> "But I didn't feel proud of where I worked. I didn't feel connected to the purpose of the company. I didn't feel connected to the mission."

As startup founders, we care deeply about what we're working on. Even if we think we're looking for stability, showing up to do a 9 to 5 job that we don't particularly care about will drive us crazy soon enough.

The conclusion Monica took from her experience working for a large insurer was that she needed a better employer, a business on a mission she cared about. Like many founders looking to find their place in the corporate world, Monica struggled to fit in.

A generalist role that leveraged her experience in the insurance industry turned out to be the role Monica was looking for when a headhunter reached out to her. Today, she is a Head of Insurance at a neobank, a senior GM role in a company she's been inspired by and a customer of for years. Reflecting on her change of career trajectory from being a founder CEO to being a GM at a bank, Monica said:

> "As a founder, you don't have that many people you can learn from. You get quite rounded experience when you're part of a business, particularly at a senior level where you're working with incredibly seasoned, experienced individuals across Product or People or Ops. That experience means that I'll be better equipped if I want to build another company again."

The financial certainty of working for a large business should not be underestimated. As founders, we rarely prioritise our financial situation; instead, we give everything to the business. Founder salaries rarely catch up with the market before Series B and sometimes not until the business is at the Series C stage. Yet, the frugality single founders in their twenties are willing to put up with often gives way to financial prudence and long-term planning as we start families and assume additional responsibilities.

For Monica, it was clear she was in a different phase of her life:

> "I don't think there should be any taboo for a founder to transition into corporate. Often, that transition can be quite transformational for someone's life. I paid myself a nominal salary during the entire startup journey. I didn't even realise the difference you feel when you get paid properly, with a pension and holidays. A lot of founders really neglect themselves. I'm quite happy that I've made that transition from quite a few angles, but definitely financially. It's a much more comfortable place to be."

Transitioning into the corporate world can be challenging for a founder trying to fit into a different culture. However, it's also an opportunity to have a significant impact, learn from seasoned professionals and be well-compensated for our efforts.

Monica isn't the only founder who found plenty of upside in working for a large business. Today, a year after choosing a corporate job, Ilana feels very differently about working at Ocado:

> "My skill sets were really quite broadly recognised; I got loads of praise, which I haven't had in years. And I continue to get that praise and make a positive impact. People were really interested in my startup experience, and I had a level of respect that, maybe, I haven't given myself.
>
> Actually, what's interesting about Ocado is that they really value doers. They like that I have done something from the ground up."

This isn't surprising. Often, when we're going through a significant transition, it may be hard to imagine what a different life might feel like. The idea of working for a corporation might bring up feelings of embarrassment, only for them to be dispelled once we have the experience of working there.

It can also go the other way. Leaving a startup, we might fantasise about how easy and pleasant it might be to work for a big company where we don't have to worry about making payroll, someone else is responsible for running sales, and we don't have to think about investor sentiment, shutting down our laptop at 5 pm.

The truth is that the reality of working for a large company is likely to be neither as horrible nor as easy as we might imagine. Whether it's the right step for us is our choice to make.

Finding the right opportunity might be challenging, but as entrepreneurs, we're a resourceful bunch. We've seen more significant challenges building our companies than landing a job. It may be challenging, but not impossible.

JOINING SOMEONE ELSE'S STARTUP

Vanessa left her startup strongly determined not to start another VC-backed company. She learned she could do it over the years of running her business. However, she wasn't keen on doing it again now that she had a small child to raise and a new sense of life priorities. A natural decision was to try to join an existing startup, which could benefit from her skills while offering some stability.

Reflecting on her journey after she found a position as a Chief of Staff at a late-stage startup, she described the process of landing that position as a "full-time job":

> "It took me a full seven months, close to 150 applications across LinkedIn and just connections, probably in excess of 30 calls with recruitment agents, VC platform partners and just introductions to get me a job interview, have an offer and accept that offer.
>
> The challenge was that I went into my startup as a specialist, but I exited it as a generalist, having led and built product, engineering and sales teams and scaled operations across UK, US, New Zealand and Europe."

Vanessa's experience highlights the same problem that founders looking for a corporate job face: they don't fit neatly into existing job specifications. In a buoyant job market, this might not be such an issue, but Vanessa happened to be looking for a job in early 2023 when the UK job market wasn't doing great:

> "There was lots of amazing talent because of recent

> restructuring at large companies, so it was a competitive market. I'd go to a LinkedIn job for, say, a Chief Operating Officer, and there were already 200 applications in the first four hours. It was like throwing an application into a big, big, dark pool. I found my job by hustling as if I were fundraising and approaching a founder who just raised and saw that they didn't have a chief of staff. I found their email and pitched myself."

When we choose an entrepreneur's career, we decide to walk an uncertain path even after we stop running our companies. We step away from the promised safety of a corporate ladder (if it exists anymore) and commit to charting our own path, whether leading our own businesses or working for someone else. Sometimes, we discover that being on someone else's senior team has more advantages than we might have thought.

Nic Yeeles, a founder who stepped down as CEO after he sold his business, Peg, eventually found his calling in being the right-hand man of the founder CEO at another company. However, just like for many other founders, the transition was not straightforward.

Realising that he was not ready to start another business, Nic decided to stay in the startup world by joining someone else's team. His first hurdle to overcome was an identity crisis, getting used to the idea that he could be working for someone else in principle. He has never done anything other than running his own businesses.

However, there were other things to overcome. The second big challenge was choosing how to position himself and proving he could do the product leadership role he sought. To get the job he wanted, Nic had to position himself carefully and then fake it till he made it:

> "I thought, Well, I'm not going to be able to walk straight into that role. You need ten years as a Product Manager. But after five or six crazy interviews, I won the job.
>
> I had to rebrand myself. I went back through my LinkedIn and changed everything to be product-related. It was fine-tuned to make it look like my entire career had been building up to this moment.
>
> I then had to 'fake it till you make it.' I remember my first week at one company; they wanted to switch to a squad structure. And I was like, I don't know what a squad is!"

However, the biggest lesson Nic learned during his transition from a founder CEO to a VP of Product (he's in his third VP Product role right now) is that his real value lies in his experience as an ex-CEO:

> "No matter how amazing the rest of the executive team is, no one else has been through the same experience that a founder CEO has. No one else thinks of the company holistically in the same way. They tend to be really good at marketing or really good at sales, but I was thinking like the CEO.
>
> As founders, we massively undervalue ourselves. However, I found that in all three companies I've worked at, I quickly became the trusted right-hand person to the CEO because no one else had my founder CEO experience.
>
> The CEO instantly trusted me, almost like another co-founder. It fits the perfect sweet spot for me where I am getting to feel like I am running a company again. But I don't have the responsibilities I had when I was a CEO."

There's a lesson here. When we, as ex-founder CEOs, try to find a job, we feel like we're unemployable, that we don't fit in, that we don't speak the language of recruiters and headhunters who are looking for VPs of Product with ten years of experience in product management. However, Nic's experience helped him realise how he was undervaluing himself.

Like getting a job in a large corporation, getting a senior position at a startup will require ingenuity to win over people with deep functional expertise. Remembering that some CEOs prize our experience as a startup CEO can be helpful.

Another lesson in these stories is that for founders looking for a job, personal connections matter precisely because, on paper, the match between the person and the role may not be obvious. Nic joined the company he's now in because he got to know the founder over the years. Both are part of Foundrs, a community of ambitious entrepreneurs, where they had a chance to build a social connection over many years.

We may also need to try our luck and pitch ourselves for positions that don't exist, like Vanessa did, making a successful argument that she'd be an outstanding Chief of Staff, or rebrand ourselves to give the impression that our entire careers led us to this moment, like Nic did.

BECOMING AN INVESTOR

Monica, a founder we met earlier in this chapter, made a dozen angel investments, started advising Entrepreneur First companies and entertained an offer to become a partner at an early-stage investment fund after she sold her startup. Having noticed that while in the US many investors have a background as operators, in the UK many investors are finance professionals, it was tempting for Monica to think she'd have an edge in choosing the best investments.

Ironically, precisely because she's an entrepreneur, she got tired of quickly looking at one investment deck after another and saying "no" to almost all of them. While the idea of being an investor might have seemed glamorous to her, the reality of the day-to-day job was far less exciting than actually building things herself.

An investment job should be taken seriously or not taken at all, lest it becomes a respectable form of gambling. The odds of failure at an early stage are so high that the overwhelming majority of investments in early-stage startups lose money. The rare successes, however, can be so big that they make up for all the losses. Therefore, to find out if your investments are any good, you need to commit to seeing thousands of decks, investing in dozens of startups each year and doing it for a few years before you have enough data to judge your performance.

If you see yourself doing this for the next decade of your life and you have an unfair advantage in the form of a broad network or a deep understanding of a particular vertical that can give you an edge, it could be an excellent opportunity for you.

You will also be paying it forward for the ecosystem. Unlike the US, Europe doesn't yet have a vibrant community of founders who invest in early-stage entrepreneurs as angels. Funds like Plural Platform, led by Ian Hogarth CBE and other exceptionally successful entrepreneurs, are rare and welcome exceptions in the investment industry dominated by finance professionals.

If you become an investor after leaving your CEO role, go for it and help fund the next generation of unicorns!

FREELANCING AS A CONSULTANT, ADVISOR OR A COACH

Many founders who leave their startups choose freelance careers to leverage two critical assets that they have: their skills and their network. However, the reasons founders choose this path differ a lot.

When I speak to founders who choose this route, they fall into one of two camps: those who see freelancing as a stop-gap solution and those who see it as the next chapter of their careers.

Either is fine. As we explored above, founders who leave their companies before the exit are rarely wealthy. Offering their services to others can be a relatively easy sale based on the strength of their network and the reputation they built in the startup community.

However, while finding a few initial contracts comes relatively easy to some, freelancing comes with a cost: relatively high day rates come with the need to sell your services.

For other founders who choose this route, including me, it's a deliberate, long-term choice rather than a holding pattern. Even since I had my first group coaching experience at CEO Bootcamp in Colorado run by Jerry Colonna and his team from Reboot, an executive coaching firm, I couldn't stop thinking that one day I could train as a coach myself.

I was there with a dozen other CEOs. We sat in a circle in a spacious room as Jerry skilfully led the conversation. It seemed like he was doing hardly anything at all, yet the energy in the room was palpable. Many of us in that room remember that retreat as a turning point in our professional growth. I remember wondering what was happening because I had no words for it.

Now I know: Jerry loved each and every one of us, including

our insecurities and fears, our dreams and desires, and he loved all of his shadow parts, too. He was fully present, and he cared.

That experience later inspired me to work with several other founder coaches and eventually train as a coach myself, supporting other founders as they navigate the entrepreneurial journey's ups and downs.

These days, when I'm contacted by other founders who are considering training as coaches or entering advisory, mentoring, or consulting, I encourage them to approach it as a long-term game, the next stage of their careers.

There's nothing wrong with making a short-term consulting contract or two if they're easy to find while you're figuring out the long-term plan, but to become good at what you do, to make it a sustainable endeavour that brings you joy, to understand what your unique gifts and talents are, to master the craft will take years. This is no different to any other profession: becoming good at your craft will take thousands of hours of deliberate practice.

And the rewards are tremendous. Serial entrepreneur François Mazoudier owned or jointly built eight companies. Then, as a corporate finance broker, he raised over $200M for his clients and learned plenty of lessons. Instead of retiring, he put everything he knew about fundraising into Fundraising Bootcamp, an intensive programme for entrepreneurs that has received rave reviews since its inception.

I love that François found a scalable way to share his deep sector knowledge, including all the mishaps, mistakes, misjudgements, and the rest, which makes it so invaluable for the next generation of European startup entrepreneurs. In doing so, he's making hundreds of founders much more likely to succeed.

For François, this decision came after realising that he needed to make a radical change from gaining knowledge to sharing knowledge to keep growing and flourishing.

One less obvious aspect of this path that some founders considering this route miss is that being good at what you do and being good at selling what you do are different skills. It's possible to be a good mentor or advisor and struggle to find people to work with. You need to master both disciplines.

An important aspect to consider when deciding to go down that path is that not being full-time with the business might have inherent limitations. It's much easier to trust a colleague who's showing up every day, just like everyone else, than an external consultant or an advisor who might not stick around to see the consequences of their work.

There is nothing wrong with fractional engagement or part-time work. Yet, if you're keen to get your hands dirty, understand the business deeply, and feel the joys (and the sorrows) of building great products together in a closely knit team, you might want to consider going full-time instead of choosing a freelance career.

Whether this path is right for you depends on what you learned about yourself as you reflected on your reasons for stepping down as the CEO of your own business. If supporting others is what you are meant to be doing, you'll build a great career there and make the ecosystem better. If you see it as an opportunity to make easy money with a high day rate, it might not turn out to be the dream career you're looking for.

BECOMING AN EXECUTIVE CHAIRPERSON

Just like every CEO job is different, there's a great degree of flexibility in what founders do if they become executive chairs of their own businesses after they step down as CEO. However, at the heart of it is the shift away from operational responsibilities towards focusing on high-level strategic questions.

This role can be a powerful platform for exploring new markets, exit opportunities, technologies, or business models without the distractions of running the business.

Jeff Lynn stepped into the role of the executive chairman to focus on board governance, exploring bold new ideas for the business and supporting the new CEO.

What made the executive chairperson position work well for Jeff and his business was clearly delineated responsibilities between him and the new CEO, as well as Jeff's prior experience as a chairman and non-executive director at various other companies.

Sometimes, the chairperson title is a respectable placeholder for the founder to determine their next steps. There's nothing wrong with this as long as the founder is honest about this with themselves and with fellow board members.

One reason that founders aren't always the most obvious choice for the chair role is that the critical responsibility of a chair is ensuring that the board is run well. This experience usually comes from serving on multiple boards over the years, which few founders who are busy running their businesses have (Jeff Lynn is an exception here).

A good chairperson also needs to be impartial and equally respect the interests of all board members and all stakeholders. This may be difficult for a founder who, until recently, led the business and likely remains a significant shareholder.

Just like every CEO's job is different, so is every chairperson's. It may be the right next step for the founder if they remain committed to the business but believe someone else needs to be in the CEO seat. Like every other aspect of the CEO succession, there's no right or wrong answer here. You'll need to decide for yourself.

This chapter outlines the seven most common career paths that follow a CEO transition, but your choice is nearly infinite. The joy and privilege of going on the founder's journey is not simply an opportunity to make a meaningful amount of money. It is also an opportunity to learn the lessons that are only available to us when we choose to navigate uncertainty, face difficulties, work under intense pressure, and endure high stakes.

I invite you to approach this next stage of your professional life not simply as a job and not even as a career but as an opportunity to find your true calling. Then, the story of running your startup that has just ended will truly be the beginning of something even greater.

Questions to reflect on:

- Which career options align most with your skills, passions, and values?
- How do your rational analysis and intuition align regarding your career choices?
- Who embodies the professional success or personal fulfilment you aspire to?
- What would you like to do professionally even if you weren't paid for it?
- How do you understand the distinction between a job, career, and calling?

FINAL THOUGHTS

Nearly a decade ago, a leading financial publication in the UK published an article about four things a CEO must always lie about. The first commandment was to never admit to not enjoying the job. I remember reading this and thinking that this advice was misguided and outdated. There's no point in endless complaining, but failing to admit how we feel to others is not an example of good modern leadership.

Instead, if we are not enjoying the job as a CEO, we must be able to discuss it openly with our boards or other entrepreneurs. It will not make us look weak. On the contrary, it takes tremendous strength to be vulnerable in front of others and explore difficult topics together. If we don't find the courage to meet our feelings and honestly look at our circumstances, we will either stay feeling trapped in our jobs or quit for reasons that we don't fully understand, feeling adrift professionally.

The right and brave thing for any founder CEO not enjoying their job to do is to look at their circumstances and their feelings with compassion, resolving to do what's needed without lying to themselves or others.

I also remember that around that time — about ten years ago

— it seemed like every founder, including me, had to pretend they were "killing it". At networking events, everyone seemed to have a story about a recent funding round they closed or a brilliant hire they just made. No one spoke about how they felt inside. I remember feeling as if I were the only founder who actually found running their startup difficult.

Over time, thankfully, this changed. As a founder community, I noticed that we learned to be a bit more open in public, acknowledging that it's not always easy. In fact, it's pretty hard at times to run a startup. Saying this openly doesn't make anyone a bad founder. Quite the contrary, these days, we are instinctively suspicious of leaders who aren't willing or able to show vulnerability. Being willing to be open with others and being emotionally intelligent is now rightly seen as important as being smart for a leader.

Today, the same needs to happen with founder CEO transitions. Taking the startup to the point where bringing someone else to run it makes sense is a mark of success, not failure. You may or may not be the best person to be the leader for the next few years. That doesn't matter. It doesn't neglect the work already done to take your company from an idea to this point.

To successfully navigate this transition, you will need to make many rational decisions, but for the most important ones, you'll need to listen to your heart. That part of yourself might not be able to offer any logical arguments, but it remembers that you're a human being with dreams and fears, carrying the capacity for both joy and suffering within you. Your heart can gently guide you towards what's right if you slow down enough for its voice to be heard.

I hope this book will help make a CEO transition less lonely if you are going through it and increase your chances of success. Too often, this subject isn't even raised except within a small circle of close friends or family. I hope this book will lead to more conversations in the entrepreneurial community about what it's truly like to go through such a transition.

Finally, I hope that the experience of navigating the CEO succession as a founder allows you to learn valuable lessons about yourself that will serve you for the rest of your life. The real promise of CEO succession isn't simply a change of leadership but an opportunity to learn who you are, discover what you're meant to be doing and face your fears.

Above all, it's an opportunity to get in touch with that deep place inside your heart that always remembers you are unconditionally human.

REFERENCES

BOOKS:

Palmer, P. J. (2000). Let Your Life Speak: Listening for the Voice of Vocation. San Francisco, CA: Jossey-Bass.

Chödrön, P. (2016). When Things Fall Apart: Heart Advice for Difficult Times. Boston: Shambhala.

Hollis, J. (2009). Through the Dark Wood: Finding Meaning in the Second Half of Life. New York: Sounds True.

Horowitz, B. (2014). The Hard Thing About Hard Things: Building a Business When There Are No Easy Answers. New York: Harper Business.

Feld, B. (2022). Startup Boards: A Field Guide to Building and Leading an Effective Board of Directors. Second Edition. Hoboken, NJ: John Wiley & Sons, Inc.

Colonna, J. (2019). Reboot: Leadership and the Art of Growing Up. New York: HarperOne.

Blumberg, M. (2020). Startup CEO: A Field Guide to Scaling Up Your Business. Second Edition. Hoboken, NJ: John Wiley & Sons, Inc.

Blumberg, M., (2021). Startup CXO: How to Build & Scale Your Executive Leadership Team. Hoboken, NJ: John Wiley & Sons, Inc.

Merckelbach, S. (2020). A Little Red Book About Source: Wisdom from 20 Years of Working with Entrepreneurs and Investors. Aquilae Verlag.

Nixon, T. (2020). Work With Source: Realise Big Ideas, Organise for Emergence and Work Artfully with Money. Gumroad.

WEBSITES:

Seedrs Academy (2023, March 13). How do You Know When it's Time to Step Down as Founder CEO?
https://www.seedrs.com/academy/how-do-you-know-when-its-time-to-step-down-as-founder-ceo

Wilson, F. (2010, August 1). What a CEO Does. AVC.
https://avc.com/2010/08/what-a-ceo-does/

Savage, T. (2018, April 5). A Founder, Not a CEO. Medium.
https://medium.com/swlh/can-we-please-stop-calling-founders-ceos-da8757b11a5a

Variety (2020, September 18). Jo Malone Slams Her Former Brand Over John Boyega Fiasco.
https://www.glossy.co/podcasts/jo-malone-on-her-second-act-jo-loves-i-wanted-to-sit-at-the-banquet-of-opportunity/

Foundrs, a Community of Ambitious Entrepreneurs:
http://www.foundrs.co

Nixon, T. Work With Source: A Blog by Tom Nixon.
https://workwithsource.com/

ACKNOWLEDGEMENTS

This book wouldn't exist without the support of so many. Only when I started writing this section did I realise how many people have supported me on this journey.

I thank Adele Barlow, my editor, for supporting me through every step of the publishing journey. Just like every book has an author, every book needs an editor. Only those who have seen my early drafts will truly appreciate how much better the book became once Adele started guiding my writing.

I offer my deep gratitude to Jerry Colonna, an executive coach who inspired me to start learning the art of radical self-inquiry. It's by asking deep questions and looking inside that we grow. Thank you for showing me the way, Jerry.

This book wouldn't have existed without Claudia Harris OBE, the CEO who took over from me at Makers. Navigating this transition together with Claudia inspired me to share what I learned with others. One morning, as Claudia and I were discussing what I might do after stepping down as CEO, she said, "Maybe you should write a book!" Two years later, Claudia was one of the first people to see the book's outline.

I'm deeply grateful to Elena Belkina, my English teacher, who taught me the language from the basics, patiently correcting my mistakes with a red pen and giving me audiotapes to listen to. Back then, as a teenager, I would have found it hard to believe I would write a book in English one day!

I am very grateful to Lucy West for encouraging me to retrain as a coach and for being my first supervisor and a great friend.

Much of what I know about CEO transitions I learned from my clients, some of whom prefer to stay anonymous. You know who you are. Thank you.

Any CEO transition journey properly undertaken touches on a spiritual dimension. I'm deeply grateful to the meditation teachers I had the good fortune to learn from: Vince and Emily Horn, Burgs and Culadasa. Like any journey, a spiritual journey needs good guides. I am lucky to have worked with them.

I would like to thank Rob Johnson, my co-founder, without whom I wouldn't have started Makers and who gave me early feedback and encouragement for this book.

I am grateful to my Makers board of directors: Claudia Harris OBE, Nic Brisbourne, Ruben Kostucki, and Litzie Maarek. Many of the most important lessons I share in the book I learned as we navigated my own CEO transition together. Thank you.

This book is a compilation of wisdom that founders, investors and operators shared with me in private conversations and who gave feedback on the draft: Jeff Lynn, Darren Ryemill, James Routledge, Dan Murray-Serter, Dave Bailey, Kim Nilsson, Omar Habbal, Rob O'Donovan, Jules Walters, Sam Knight, Tom Savage, Arvinda Gohil, Kate Glazebrook, Rory Stirling, Jon Lerner, Eugene Tsyrklevich, Ian Walker, Victoria Rusnac, Christina Nesheva, Adrian Shedden, Alex Depledge, Anatolij

Dzjuba, Ashley Friedlein, Ben Dodd, Ben Henley-Smith, David Brookes, Matt Celuzak, Charlie Walker, Christoph Lippuner, Diane Freymond, Elspeth Coates, François Mazoudier, Guillaume Bouchard, Henrik Hagemann, Ilana Lever, Jamie Undrell, James McAulay, Anaïs Leon, Mac Piskorz, Maksim Sipos, Nic Yeeles, Phoebe Hugh, Ramakrishna Nanjundaiah, Richard Hurtley, Sam Conniff, Sarah Brooks, Seb Isaacs, Simon Wakeman, Simon Overell, Tess Cosad, Tushar Agarwal, Weiting Liu, Eloi Pecquet, Mark Ramondt, Abbie Morris, Daniel Endler, Christian Kerr, Ilya Brotzky, Arunjay Katakam, Øyvind Reed, Gemma Goodacre, Liam Young, Varun Bhanot, Gideon Chain, Kate Pljaskokova, Peter Nixey, Zoë Desmond, Dan Land, Henry Coutinho-Mason, Rabin Yaghoubi, Ed Dowding, Douglas de Jager, Gabbi Cahane, Georgina Harding, Tim Armoo, Seb Blanc, Noah Abelson-Gertler, Noah Geeves, Hannah Feldman, Jim Clear, Elin Ng, Adam Fudakowski, Erich Nussbaumer, Amy Golding, Ben Jones, Irra Ariella Khi, Matt Lerner, Emma Brown, Maddy Cross, Tom Nixon, Simon La Fosse, Leila Zegna, Rod Banner, Kyrill Zlobenko, Azeem Azhar, Gi Fernando MBE, Tom Robins, Peter Ward, Martin Fincham, Sarah Ellis and many others. I am grateful to each and every one of you.

I would like to thank Chris Grew of Orrick, who taught me the basics of fundraising negotiations. The lessons I learned from Chris stayed with me for years and served many of my clients well, too.

I'm grateful to my coach, Krish Surroy, who has supported me throughout this book's writing process. Every coach needs a coach, and I'm very grateful for the opportunity to work with Krish.

I would like to express gratitude to Gretchen Lennon of Lennon Legal, a legal services firm for early-stage companies, who helped me understand some finer legal points I needed to write this book.

Needless to say, this book wouldn't have existed without my parents, Irina and Vitaliy, and my sister, Lena, who always believed in me and supported me regardless of what I've been going through. Thank you!

I owe a debt of gratitude to Foundrs, an incredible community of entrepreneurs, many of whom shared their stories and hard-earned lessons in late-night, off-the-record conversations. I'm so grateful to all of you.

Thank you, Leo Feldman, for giving me a sense of perspective when I was tired after working on the draft all day.

Without a doubt, I forgot many people who helped and supported me during the process of writing this book. For this, I apologise. My forgetfulness is mine alone.

Finally, I would like to thank my fiancée, Egle Vilutyte, for her unwavering and unconditional support as I've navigated my career as a coach and, now, as an author. Your support and love means more than you'll ever know.

ABOUT THE AUTHOR

After stepping down as the founder CEO of Makers, one of the UK's leading coding bootcamps, Evgeny Shadchnev became a certified professional coach specialising in helping entrepreneurs through CEO succession.

He now guides founders and boards through the complex personal, professional, and psychological terrain when the stakes are highest. His insightful strategies prepare entrepreneurs to confidently navigate the transition from founder CEO to a new CEO.

As a meditation teacher in training, he enjoys a simple and quiet lifestyle in southern Portugal.

Read more about the author here: https://www.evgeny.coach

Printed in Poland
by Amazon Fulfillment
Poland Sp. z o.o., Wrocław
07 May 2024

fd756449-6a62-44eb-862b-95e69b20ea33R01